# Things Fail People Fall

## Getting up
## and going on with life
## after you've ~~failed~~ *fallen*

Deborah P. Brunt

New Hope
Birmingham, Alabama

Published by:
New Hope
P.O. Box 12065
Birmingham, Alabama 35202-2065

Cover design by Barry Graham

Bible verses taken from:
King James Version

Excerpts from the New American Standard Bible: Copyright © 1960, 1962,
1963, 1968, 1971, 1972, 1973, 1975, 1977 by The Lockman Foundation.
A corporation not for profit, La Habra CA. All rights reserved,
printed in the United States of America. Used by permission.

Holy Bible, New International Version. Copyright© 1973, 1978, 1984
International Bible Society. Used by permission of Zondervan Bible Publishers.

*Good News Bible,* Today's English Version (TEV):
Used by permission, American Bible Society. Copyright © 1976.

Dewey Decimal Classifications: 248.6
Subject Headings: CHRISTIAN LIFE
                  PSYCHOLOGY, APPLIED
                  FAILURE (PSYCHOLOGY)
                  FAILURE (PSYCHOLOGY)--MORAL AND RELIGIOUS ASPECTS

ISBN: 1-56309-014-7
N914104 ■ 5M ■ 0691

▼▼▼▼▼▼▼

# Contents

▼▼▼▼▼▼▼

# Introduction:
# The End

I had cried for three days. Someone else might have shrugged off the news I'd just heard. But to me, it was devastating.

The previous fall, I had agreed to co-teach a tenth- and eleventh-grade girls' Sunday School class. Before making the decision, I prayed and searched God's Word for a go-ahead. One morning during my daily quiet time, I read Psalm 23:3: "He guides me in the paths of righteousness for His name's sake" (NAS). I felt God's Spirit nudge me. His answer, I firmly believed, was yes.

On accepting the class, I promised the Lord I'd give myself 100 percent to my ministry there.

Dee (my co-teacher) and I were to divide both teaching and outreach responsibilities. (Our department director hoped that during the year the class would grow and form two classes.)

The two of us decided we would alternate teaching every other unit. We felt that approach would give cohesiveness to the lessons. Because we both had preschoolers—and we never knew when a child might wake up sick on Sunday morning—we agreed to be ready to fill in for each other on any given Sunday.

We divided the roll by grade level. Dee took the sophomores; I took the juniors. Privately, I committed myself to call each girl on my roll once every two weeks.

Through that phone calling ministry, God allowed me to minister to the girls who never darkened the church doors. One girl on roll had attended our Sunday School with a friend but was a member of a nonevangelical denomination. Asking her permission to keep her on my prayer and phone calling list, I built a relationship with her and was able to tell her what it means to receive Jesus Christ as Lord.

Another girl whom I never met in person began confiding in me almost from the first phone call. She told me some of the deep problems in her troubled home situation: her parents were divorced; she was using drugs. The third time I called her, she also told me she was pregnant and planning to have an abortion.

For several weeks, I counseled her (I could not convince her to go to a Christian crisis pregnancy center) and agonized in prayer for her unborn baby. Eventually, she did abort the baby. I continued to call the girl, to pray for her, and to witness to her, even while I grieved for her unborn child.

On Sunday mornings, I could feel resistance when I taught. That bothered me, but I had felt friction before when teaching youth, so I turned that resistant spirit over to the Lord and asked Him to overcome it.

What bothered me far more were the problems Dee and I were having. She had surprised me one Sunday evening during an altar call by coming to me and confessing jealousy of me. I had been a Christian longer than she, she said. I had taught youth in another church for several years. I was writing Sunday School lessons for youth, to be published by our denomination's publishing house.

Yet, Dee had her own strengths. Her outgoing, bubbly personality made it easy for her to relate to the girls. She had good ideas for class get-togethers and the energy to implement them.

I had thought our differences would be an asset. We would complement each other. After Dee's confession, though, our working together became increasingly harder.

Finally, one Sunday in February, I showed up for Sunday School on a morning Dee was supposed to teach. While I was chatting with some of the girls, another youth Sunday School teacher appeared at our doorway. She said, "Dee called me last night. One of her girls is sick. She asked if your class could come in with mine for the lesson today."

Stunned and angry, I thanked her but said that I would teach my class.

The next day, I phoned Dee. "Why didn't you let me know you couldn't come to Sunday School yesterday, Dee? I was prepared to fill in. That's one of the main reasons for our co-teaching."

After offering several excuses, all of which I batted down, Dee said, "Well, I didn't want to tell you this."

"Tell me what?" I asked, puzzled.

"The girls don't like your teaching."

For the second time in two days, I was stunned. Later that afternoon, I called our department director. Some of the girls in the class had told him the same thing several months earlier. Their complaints? I'd asked them to wear name tags the first Sunday I taught. I tried to use methods other than straight lecture to help them learn. The eleventh graders in the class felt that doing activities in Sunday School was juvenile.

They had told Dee. They had told our department director. But no one had told me. I was humiliated, wondering who else had been talking about how bad a youth Sunday School teacher I was.

I was also devastated. I cried for three days. Emotionally, I was on tilt, anyway. Just the week before, I'd discovered that I was pregnant with my second child. The news thrilled me, but the changes my body was experiencing made the tears flow more easily.

On a deeper level, I agonized because I had met what I had thought to be impossible. I'd met failure in a ministry to which I believed God had called me and into which I had wholly poured myself, by His grace.

I knew I wasn't outgoing like Dee, but I did feel God had given me the ability to teach. I had asked Him before each session what truths to emphasize and how to emphasize them. Each week, I had prayed by name for the girls in the class. I'd reached out through phone calls and cards and tried to minister to them, as God led. And I'd failed.

Unanswered questions ran, over and over, through my mind: Did I misunderstand You, God, in taking the class? Did I fail each Sunday to hear Your directions for leading the girls? If so, how can I know I haven't misunderstood in other areas where I've tried to follow Your leading?

Lord God, if I can't hear clearly what You're telling me to teach youth, what in the world am I doing writing youth Sunday School lessons? Is the material I've written as far off target as my classroom teaching seems to have been?

And, Lord, what do I do now? If the problem involved just the girls and me, I believe I could regroup, dig in, and start over. But, in my pregnant condition, I don't know if I can cope with the struggle to relate to both my fellow teacher and my pupils.

As I prayed for God to show me what to do, I wondered how I would know His answer.

# QUESTIONING

During the days that followed, I wanted to focus on the wrong everyone else had done to me. But, in seeking to know what had happened, I had to ask, "Lord, how have I failed You?"

As I prayed for God's perspective, He showed me two things. First, He underscored a Scripture verse I read one morning, assuring me it was His word to me: "They will know that a prophet has been in their midst" (Ezek. 33:33 NAS).

At the same time, He convicted me that I had been guilty of pride. I had allowed fleeting but deadly proud thoughts to go undealt with. I'd noticed those thoughts vaguely, but had not faced them and confessed them.

God reminded me that in my late teens, pride had led me into open rebellion against Him.

# REMEMBERING

I accepted Jesus as Lord when I was eight years old. I had grown in Him through elementary school, junior high, and most of high school. By graduation time, however, pride had gotten a foothold on me. I could not see my sins for what they were. I only saw the "good things" I was doing for God.

I went off to my freshman year at a state university and, spiritually speaking, fell flat on my face. Early in the first semester, I began a dating relationship I should never have gotten into. My boyfriend, Brad, was not a Christian and had no desire to be one. In my pride, I thought I could "win" him and his friends to Jesus.

I didn't know 1 Corinthians 15:33: "Do not be deceived: `Bad company corrupts good morals'" (NAS). Even if I had known that verse, I probably would have disregarded it.

Before long, I was involved in sins that had never before tempted me. My pride had turned into rebellion. I didn't know anymore whether God was real, yet I felt the prickings of His Holy Spirit daily. I was miserable.

For nearly two years, I stubbornly pursued my own way. Then, the summer before my junior year, God pushed me back on track.

I was working at Walt Disney World in Florida. I'd been sneaking into the back pews of a church in Orlando for Sunday morning services, wanting to return to God and yet hanging onto my relationship with Brad. One Sunday, the preacher spoke on repentance. His message was God's ultimatum to me.

I did repent. Going back to school in the fall, I ended my relationship with Brad. For more than a year, I didn't date at all. The Lord enabled me to rebuild my prayer life. He gave me a new hunger for His Word and helped me find Christian friends. I became active in a campus Bible study and a local church.

My desperate prayer at the time was, "Lord, make it stick. Make this new surrender to You last the rest of my life. Please don't let pride ever get a foothold in my life again."

In seeking insight into my failure as a Sunday School teacher, I realized God had answered my previous prayer quite dramatically.

## RECOVERING

God helped me recover from the failure of my college days. He has also helped me recover from failure in ministry. Through these and other situations, He has taught me the principles you will find in this book.

Of course, I still encounter failure. I'm continuing to learn how to live out the truths about which I've written. But bruises, scars, and all, I'm committed to getting up and going on in Christ.

Please, won't you come with me?

# 1

▼▼▼▼▼▼▼

# Face Downward:
# God's People Can Fail

When June walked into her new classroom, she was confident she could control the class and teach English. After all, she'd been doing those very things for years.

But she was not prepared for the utter chaos that reigned in her classes for months. Students would not do assignments she believed they could do. They moved their desks together, refused to work individually, and became angry when told to put their chairs in rows for quizzes. Though young adults, they acted like teenagers toward classmates of the opposite sex.

The male students resented taking directions from a woman. Everyone resented June's being an American.

June had taught English—mainly high school literature—in an Arab school in the Middle East for 15 years. Recently, she had agreed to spend three months teaching English to adult Arab nursing students in an Israeli-occupied land.

She was in the Middle East not only to teach, but also to share Christ with her students and their families and friends. She felt keenly her responsibility to teach well. Her teaching skills were the reason the government allowed her to live there.

June's previous students, although predominantly Muslim, had respected her authority. They had been eager to learn. Many had begun, at age three, attending the Christian school at which she taught. They had grown up relating to Christians.

June's new students were warm and outgoing outside the classroom, but angry, unmotivated, and uncontrollable inside. Most were young men. Some had been active members of pro-Arab organizations. They had grown up resenting Americans. Before coming to nursing school, they had never had female classmates or a woman teacher.

These students saw no need to learn English. They only cared about passing the course so they could finish nursing school.

To make matters worse, June did not have a textbook. She had to create materials day by day, using several English textbooks.

Yet, she was determined to teach her students what they needed to know: how to read and understand nursing material and how to write acceptable nursing plans and discussion answers on tests. Further, June was determined to put together English lessons her students would want to study.

She grew thoroughly frustrated when she failed time and again to find a level of work they could—or would—do.

June might have looked with relief on the end of her three-month commitment to the nursing school. Yet, when time came to leave, she chose to stay.

Conditions did not improve, however. In fact, they worsened. Chaos still ruled inside the classroom when events outside class began adding to June's growing sense of failure.

The events? Uprisings. Arabs in the country began to revolt openly against Israeli control. The result? Thousands of casualties started pouring into the hospital adjoining the nursing school. June's energetic, if resentful, students turned sullen, lifeless, and distracted. In time, two students were shot. Another was jailed.

Each day when June left class to walk through the hospital area to her home on campus, wounded Arabs and their families eyed her with hatred. She could not get away from the oppressive environment, even to go out to dinner, because of strict curfews. She could not call her family in the United States because the international phone lines had been cut.

She became frustrated and angry—angry with herself, as well as the students. She began to resent her pupils' actions, the situation in which she found herself, and even some of the students themselves. "This was hardly a setting for sharing my faith with them," she says.

In the midst of impossible conditions, she became so intent on teaching English that she forgot, first, to touch lives. "[The students] were the people I had come to minister to. I should have cared more about them than about anything related to English. But I failed to do that," she says.

7

June had walked into the middle of the Arab-Israeli conflict, knowing the situation would be difficult, but believing she could handle it. In a way, she was wrong. She did not handle everything well.

But in another way, she was right. By taking her failures in stride, she is learning to handle living in the place God has placed her.

Since her first months in her new teaching post, June has begun to see her students in a new light. She is learning first to love them and second to teach them. She has now established a measure of order in the classroom. She has recognized anew that all her strength and hope lie, not in her own ability, but in God's power to do far more abundantly than all she asks or thinks (see Eph. 3:20). She is trying to seize the "rare and wonderful opportunity" she has to minister and witness to Muslims.

June says, "Failure is a part of ministry. Failure is a part of living." She also believes failure must not be the end. Even in impossible situations, she says, "We will also have successes—because of Who Christ is."

## WHAT HAPPENED?

Everyone fails from time to time. Most of us shrug off small failures. In fact, we must shrug them off to stay sane. Even the most perfectionistic person must admit, "I'm human." As humans, we're going to fall short of perfection at times.

Small failures can create discouragement, however, when the same ones happen again and again. You may, for example, have tried countless times to quit a bad habit or to start a good one. You may have yelled at the children or gossiped or eaten too much—again.

Every time you fail in one of these "little" ways, your feelings of self-worth suffer. Your desire to try again erodes.

But the failures that can really paralyze are the ones you count as "biggies." Your marriage falls apart. Dreams for career or family crumble. A God-given ministry bears no fruit.

When such a failure hits, you may find yourself in a tailspin—and feel powerless to pull out of it. No longer flying along toward the goals you believed you'd someday reach, you quickly lose self-esteem and self-confidence. Doubts, anger, bitterness, and despair engulf you.

For Christians, major failures can prove especially devastating. After all, Christians are God's children, and He promises His children victory. Right?

Many in Christian circles preach that those who obey Christ will prosper materially and succeed in every undertaking. Some Scripture passages seem to back these preachers up. Psalm 1, for example, proclaims, "Happy are those who . . . find joy in obeying the Law of the Lord. . . . They succeed in everything they do" (vv. 1-3 TEV).

In light of these teachings, believers who have met defeat often feel branded. They're weighted down by the feeling that, to have failed so soundly, they must somehow have sinned greatly.

# WHERE DOES SIN FIT IN?
## A Principle
God's Word does predict ruin for those who do evil. Consider, for example, Proverbs 11:5: "A wicked man will cause his own downfall" (TEV).

The Bible also gives God's people promises of victory, dependent on their obeying Him: "The righteous will prosper like the leaves of summer" (Prov. 11:28 TEV).

Adam and Eve were the first to test this sin-leads-to-failure principle. They found it to be true. In doing what God had expressly forbidden, the two lost their Garden home, their close walk with God, their innocence, and their carefree lives. They faced homelessness, hard labor, grief, and death.

Moses, David, and Peter also experienced failures as a result of sin. Today, people still meet defeats due to sin.

One government leader recently failed to complete his first term in an elected office. He had previously held two other positions. In each, he had been suspected of shady dealings. Although a church member, he had not attended church services in years. Setting out to get elected to his third—and most influential—post, he advertised, "I believe in God."

He was elected. Three years later, he was convicted of a felony and forced to resign.

## A Precept
What, then, does it mean when a Christian suffers a major defeat? Are the prosperity teachers right? Will the person who obeys God always have more than enough money, an ideal home life, a steadily improving career, an effective ministry, and perfect health?

Is failure always a direct result of sin? Is the extent of a failure always in direct proportion to the ugliness of the sin?

Job's friends thought so. They built lengthy speeches around their

9

belief that, because Job's family, career, wealth, and health were in shambles, he must have done some great evil.

When God was ready to speak out about the matter, he told Job's friends, "I am angry with you . . . because you did not speak the truth about Me" (Job 42:7 TEV).

God's truth involves balance. The same Lord who declared that the righteous "succeed in everything they do" (Psalm 1:3 TEV) also said, "A righteous man falls seven times, and rises again" (Prov. 24:16 NAS). This and other Bible passages acknowledge that persons truly committed to God, seeking to walk in His ways, will experience failures.

## A Story

Judges 19-20 recounts an ugly incident in the history of Israel. A man from the tribe of Levi and his concubine were traveling through the region belonging to the tribe of Benjamin. They stopped overnight at the town of Gibeah. During the night, the men of Gibeah raped and killed the Levite's concubine and tried to sexually assault the Levite.

As soon as possible, the Levite notified all Israel of what had happened. The Israelites demanded that the tribe of Benjamin turn over to them the men who had committed the atrocity. In response, the Benjamites assembled 26,700 soldiers at Gibeah to fight against their fellow countrymen.

The Israelites, in turn, gathered 400,000 trained soldiers from the other 11 tribes. They then prayed for God's guidance. The Lord gave them direction as to how to carry out the battle, and they obeyed.

The result? The "bad guys" won the battle. Before the day ended, the Benjamites had killed 22,000 Israelite soldiers.

Stunned, the Israelites mourned before the Lord until evening. They prayed, "Should we go again into battle against our Benjamite relatives?"

When the Lord answered, "Yes," the Israelite soldiers again took their positions. They marched, a second time, against Benjamin. The Benjamite army again came out of Gibeah—and won. This time, they killed 18,000 of the Israelite troops.

Then all Israel wept, fasted, and offered sacrifices to God until evening. Brokenhearted, they prayed, "Should we go out to fight the Benjamites a third time, or should we give up?"

The Lord answered, "Fight. Tomorrow I will give you victory over them" (Judg. 20:28 TEV).

That third day, the Israelites did win the battle, losing only 30 men. They annihilated the Benjamite army. But in trying to follow the Lord as best they knew how, Israel had suffered two devastating defeats, costing 40,000 lives.

Why? The Bible does not say.

God won't always tell us why we've failed, either. His Word advises, "There are some things that the Lord our God has kept secret" (Deut. 29:29 TEV).

When we ask "Why?" He may not give us enough answers to satisfy our curiosity, but He will reveal what we need to know in order to go on.

## I CAN GO ON?

To His people who have failed, God offers solid promises of recovery:

❑ "The Lord lifts those who have fallen" (Psalm 145:14 TEV).

❑ "If [those who please the Lord] fall, they will not stay down, because the Lord will help them up" (Psalm 37:24 TEV).

❑ "No matter how often an honest man falls, he always gets up again" (Prov. 24:16 TEV).

Notice that each of these verses speaks in terms, not of failing, but of falling. Almost always, in God's Word, **things** fail; **people** fall.

Why? Perhaps because the term failure carries with it a ring of finality. And, as Jeremiah wrote, "When someone falls down, doesn't he get back up?" (Jer. 8:4 TEV).

Ann was drum major of a high school band. During a Veteran's Day parade, she was leading the band down the main street of town. At her director's orders, she had turned around and was marching backwards, leading a march tune. The heel of her boot caught in a manhole cover. Before she knew what was happening, she was falling.

In the split second of her fall, she thought first: I'll just stay down, and everyone will feel sorry for me. Then she realized: If I stay down, the band will go to pieces.

Ann hit the ground, jumped back up, whirled around, and kept marching.

Doris fell in her home and broke both of the weight-bearing bones in her lower leg. She could not get up by herself. Her husband carried her to the bed. The paramedics took her to the hospital, where a doctor put a cast on the leg. In her case, jumping up and going on would have been detrimental and dangerous, if even possible.

Doris wore a cast for more than seven months. Needless to say, the fall slowed her down considerably. But in spite of the pain and the inconvenience, she did get up. She did go on.

## WHAT NOW?

Have you met failure recently? Do you know someone who has? If so, you (or your friend) may still be lying flat. That's OK. Most people would never expect someone with a broken leg to do anything but lie still until help comes. Yet many persons expect those suffering from a broken heart or a broken spirit to recover instantly.

This book is designed to help you in the recovery process. Whether you're trying to deal with your own failure or learn how to help someone else, you will find guidelines for:

❑ *glancing backward* at the factors that caused the failure;
❑ *gazing upward* at the One who alone can bring recovery;
❑ *looking inward* for new motivation to try again;
❑ *turning outward* to seek help from—and offer help to—others;
❑ and, finally, *going forward* in the power of God's Spirit.

In the pages of this book, you will meet dedicated Christian men and women who have been knocked flat by failure and who are getting up and going on. Most are now, or have been, involved in professional Christian ministry. Two have left missions fields; two have suffered severe depression; one has been in a mental institution. You will meet a pastor forced to resign his church and couples who have dealt with failure in marriage. You will encounter failed ministries. You will read about failures that cost, or almost cost, lives.

In all these accounts, you will find two common threads: (1) courage on the part of committed Christians willing to admit, "I've failed," and (2) grace from God.

My prayer is that, encouraged by the examples of these men and women, you who have been knocked down by failure will regain your own equilibrium and let God lift you up again.

# 2

▼▼▼▼▼▼▼

# Face Downward:
# I Was Tripped!

Have you ever seen someone deliberately trip another—and then take delight in the victim's embarrassment and pain? It's not a pretty scene to witness. But it happens.

## DAVID: TRIPPED BY HIS KING

In the days of Israel's first king, Saul "planned to make David fall" (1 Sam. 18:25 NAS). King Saul held the scepter, but David was receiving the acclaim. David had killed Goliath. He successfully commanded 1,000 soldiers. He had won the allegiance of Saul's son Jonathan, heir apparent to the throne. Now, Saul's daughter, Michal, loved David and wanted to marry him.

So Saul made David a proposition: "You may be my son-in-law" (1 Sam. 18:21b NAS). David had already turned down an offer of marriage to one of Saul's daughters, however. He did not think himself socially or financially worthy to marry into the king's family.

So when David seemed about to turn Saul down a second time, Saul sent his servants to convince the young commander to accept the offer. The servants told David, "All the king wants from you as payment for the bride are the foreskins of a hundred dead Philistines, as revenge on his enemies" (1 Sam. 18:25 TEV).

Wanting to marry Michal, David finally consented. He set out with his men to kill 100 Philistines.

Saul was delighted. He had, in essence, thrown his foot out in front of the unsuspecting David. He fully intended that David fall in the battle with the Philistines, Israel's enemies.

David did not fall, however. Instead, he came marching home with twice as much dowry as the king had asked.

## ISRAEL: TRIPPED BY A SEER

Earlier in Bible history, the nation Israel did not fare as well as David. When tripped, the people of God fell hard.

Camped in Moab, east of the Jordan River, the Israelites were preparing to end 40 years of wilderness wandering. Thirty-eight years earlier, standing on the brink of Canaan, they had refused to go in. This time, they intended to claim that land.

But while in Moab, the men of Israel did something God had repeatedly warned His people not to do: They became sexually involved with the pagan women of the land.

As a result, Israel fell into the worship of heathen gods. A plague snuffed out the lives of 24,000 Israelites. And God's nation came within a hair's breadth of failing, again, to claim the land of promise.

The Israelites fell because of their own unchecked desires. But a king's fear and a seer's counsel triggered their fall.

King Balak of Moab, terrified by the vast nation camped on his land, had hired a seer named Balaam to curse Israel. Balaam had made three attempts to pronounce such a curse; each time, God had turned the curse into a blessing. Balaam was sent home in disgrace. But before going he apparently stopped long enough to whisper a suggestion in King Balak's ear: "You want to destroy the Israelites? Here's what I would do. . . . "

The Israelites later killed Balaam in battle. After that battle, God reminded His people what Balaam had done to cause them such grief: "Remember that it was the [Moabite and Midianite] women who *followed Balaam's instructions* and at Peor led the people to be unfaithful to the Lord" (Num. 31:16 TEV, italics added).

## BELIEVERS: FELLED BY AN ADVERSARY

We Christians have something in common with David and the Israelites. When we fall, we do not do so by accident. God's Word promises that His angels watch us constantly to protect us from "slip-ups" (see Psalm 91:11-12).

When we fail, we can know that someone with evil intent tripped us. That someone is real, though not the flesh-and-blood persons we may be tempted to blame for our failure.

Our foes are much more formidable than either King Saul or

Balaam ever dreamed of being. Our foes "are many; And they hate [us] with violent hatred" (Psalm 25:19 NAS). Paul described them in Ephesians 6:12 as "the wicked spiritual forces in the heavenly world" (TEV).

Jesus addressed these hate-filled spiritual forces, not as nebulous energy, but as personal beings. The New Testament calls them demons. They form a vast and cruel army, led by our ultimate adversary, Satan.

Restless and tortured, Satan and his legions stay constantly on the move, "seeking someone to devour" (1 Peter 5:8 NAS). With skill, determination, and great power, they plot failures for Christians.

They keep well-hidden behind outward appearances while delivering knockout blows to unsuspecting believers. Then, when God's people go sprawling, the hosts of hell rejoice.

Certainly, God is able to protect those who are His from such attacks. Our God is almighty. Sometimes, though, He lets our adversaries through. He did so in the case of Job (see Job 1:6-12). He also did so in the life of a missionary named Jan.

## JAN: STRUCK DOWN, BUT NOT DESTROYED

Jan arrived in her Latin American missions field in 1976, eager to face the task that lay ahead. God had prepared her well for career missions.

He dealt with her at the age of eight, and she became a Christian. He "grew her up" in missions organizations in a missions-minded church. She knew she wanted to be a missionary from age 9.

The summer after her senior year in high school, Jan spent 11 weeks as an exchange student in a South American country. During her last two summers in college, she did missionary work in the United States. One of those summers, she worked with Spanish migrants.

After college graduation, Jan served a two-year missions stint in South America. While there, she realized that missionaries had shortcomings.

By the time Jan finished seminary and headed for her permanent missions field, she knew conversational Spanish, loved the Latin people, and appreciated the realities of missionary life.

She spent a year in language study, then plunged into her duties as a women's worker. For two years, her ministry was full and productive.

Then, in 1980, Jan explains, "things really blew up." That year, more than half the denomination's elected leaders in the country in which she served were under 30 years of age. Their youth, inexperience, and volatile natures led to relationship problems.

Three missionary families were attacked verbally and emotionally and told they were not wanted in the country. Two of those families left. Then came Jan's turn. She was lied about. Her actions were misrepresented. She became involved in several ugly scenes with convention leaders.

Although Jan tried every way she knew to bring about reconciliation, nothing worked. Finally, she received a telegram saying, "We think you would have a better ministry in another country."

For the five months left until her furlough, Jan did not function well. She remembers, "I was very, very down, very upset. All the missionaries were."

She came home on furlough in December 1980. During her year in the states, Jan came to understand herself better through sessions with a Christian counselor. She came to understand the situation on her missions field better by talking with a seminary professor of missions.

She headed back to the field in January 1982, feeling a little anxious, but otherwise very good about going back. She says, "I did not really realize at the time the damage that had been done to myself and to my ministry, and to my emotional state."

During the next two years, Jan tried to make up for her previous "failure." In so doing, she took on many more responsibilities than she could handle.

With far too many things to do and not nearly enough time to do them, she became frustrated and guilt-ridden. The guilt paralyzed her, throwing her farther behind in her work. She soon felt trapped in a cycle of inaction and guilt.

By February 1983, Jan was in a deep depression. She did not realize it, though. She knew she felt sad, but she thought, "I just need to pull myself together and get back to work."

Not until 11 months later did Jan talk to her supervisor about her problem. By then she could not even go to her office without crying uncontrollably and having to leave. Most of the time, she sat at home, staring at the TV or out the back door.

Jan's supervisor urged her to return to the states on medical leave. She agreed to do so.

During her year-long furlough, a doctor checked her, a counselor met with her weekly, and a psychiatrist treated her. The psychiatrist put her on a medication which she took for five months. Two weeks after taking the first dose, she woke up feeling glad to be alive for the first time in months.

After a year at home, Jan felt ready to go back. In fact, she felt she had to go back. In January 1985, she left once more for her chosen field. For the next year, she estimates she was functioning at about 75 percent potential. Afraid of getting herself trapped in another depression-causing cycle, she was sometimes too cautious of accepting responsibilities.

Then, she met another roadblock. Two church women opposed her to the point that her ministry to women in the churches stayed "pretty much at a standstill" for a year. During that year, Jan turned her attention to working with college students and starting churches.

Slowly, though, things changed. A group of leading women from the churches apologized for their two coworkers' actions and invited Jan to work with them again. Jan agreed. As the days passed, her confidence and output grew until she finally felt fully productive once more.

The last year before she was to come home again on furlough, she saw several evidences of God's hand on her ministry. A church that had opposed her during the convention troubles in 1980 came to her and begged her to work with them again. She says, "That, after eight years, was wonderful to see." Also, one of the women who had been so abusive when Jan returned to the field in 1985 began to compliment and support her work.

About March 1988, in the midst of the good things that were happening, Jan saw signs that depression was creeping up on her again. She began seeing a local psychiatrist.

She was immediately impressed with his skill and professionalism. She says, "He brought me much farther along than I had been before, as far as emotional stability and raising my self-esteem."

The psychiatrist ended his sessions with Jan in December before her scheduled furlough in January. He said that, as far as he saw, she was fine and should not have any recurrence of the depression. Then, two weeks before leaving for the states, Jan received another blow. She learned that several fellow missionaries had written negative evaluations of her work.

Jan knew her relationships with some of the missionaries were distant and, at times, discordant. But she had always respected her coworkers' ministries. Until now, she had thought they, likewise, respected hers.

17

Four months into her furlough, Jan was told she would not be going back to the missions field she had left. For the third time in nine years, she had been "struck down."

## OVERCOMERS: READY FOR AMBUSH

Question: How could three such devastating blows befall a career missionary whom God had called, prepared, and guided?

Answer: Jan was ambushed.

Law officers trying to break up a crime ring focus on catching the person at the top. The "little guys," after all, are dispensable. If picked up, they can quickly be replaced.

In trying to overcome her failures, Jan could lay blame on circumstances, on the Latin Christians, on her fellow missionaries, on herself. But she would only be pointing fingers at the "little guys." Jan's falls were engineered, ultimately, by the adversary.

Perhaps you've been ambushed, too. Even if not, you may be ambushed by powerful unseen forces at any time. Should that knowledge cause you to cower in fear and defeat? No, it should wake you up to at least four positive steps you can take to avoid and deal with failure.

*1. Stay alert.*

If you know someone's out to trip you, you can more readily avoid being tripped. The man to whom the Good Samaritan ministered would probably have changed his travel plans had he known thieves were waiting for him on the Jerusalem-to-Jericho road. You too can sidestep some direct attacks. Watch for trouble signs both within and outside yourself. Wake up to areas in which you may be compromising your Christian standards, even a little. Keep an eagle eye out for pride and presumption. Be sensitive to the attitudes and actions of those whose lives touch yours.

Barbara's husband, Barney, had accepted a new job and the family moved to a different state. Two weeks later, Barbara gave birth to the couple's second child.

Their two-year-old daughter was experiencing the "terrible twos" with a passion. With so many new things in her life, she daily threw tantrums, made her baby sister cry, or resolutely refused to do anything she was told to do. To make matters worse, Barney's job was not turning out as he had expected. He was working long hours doing tasks he did not at all enjoy. The baby seemed to pick the times he was home to cry.

Barbara suddenly realized that things were more strained between her and Barney than at any other time in their marriage. She didn't just dismiss the problem. Instead, she called a prayer partner. The two began praying fervently for God to protect the couple's marriage. Barbara also looked for ways to strengthen the bond between her and her husband.

In the weeks that followed, God did protect Barbara and Barney against the enemy forces trying to sabotage their marriage. By the time Barney changed jobs again several months later, the couple's relationship was stronger than it had been before the crisis.

If Barbara had not realized what was happening, her story might have had the same ending as did the story of the biblical general, Abner.

After King Saul's death, Abner stayed loyal to Saul's son, Ishbosheth, until Ishbosheth accused him of adultery. Then a furious General Abner decided to throw his support to David (then king of the tribe of Judah only).

On learning of Abner's defection, David's top general, Joab, called Abner aside, pretending to want to speak to him privately. Then Joab stabbed the defecting soldier. (A threat to Joab's position, Abner had also killed Joab's brother in battle.) David lamented for Abner, "As one falls before the wicked, you have fallen" (2 Sam. 3:34b NAS).

Abner fell because he did not recognize Joab as the enemy. He was not on the alert against attack. God's Word urges, "Be alert, be on watch! Your enemy, the Devil, roams around like a roaring lion, looking for someone to devour" (1 Peter 5:8 TEV).

### 2. Know when you've been attacked.

Don't dismiss the devil and his demons as biblical myth. When you've fallen before evil spiritual forces, admit it.

In Matthew 13, Jesus told a parable about a man who sowed good seed in his field. When the seed began to sprout, however, the man found weeds growing right alongside the good grain. His servants asked, "Sir, it was good seed you sowed in your field; where did the weeds come from?" The man, though he had not seen what had happened, knew the source of the trouble: "'It was some enemy who did this,' he answered" (Matt. 13:27, 28 TEV).

Becky recently served on the second pastor search committee her church had organized in one year. The first committee had dissolved itself after its members could not come to an agreement on a man to present to the church.

From the first meeting of the second committee, each of the six very different members recognized a special oneness they had in common. They committed themselves to prayer as their first and most important approach in seeking a pastor. They asked for input from church leaders and members. They regularly updated the church on their progress.

After several months, the committee unanimously recommended a man to serve as pastor. The church welcomed him for a "trial sermon" weekend. The following Sunday, church members voted *not* to call him.

For the whole committee, the hurt was numbing—especially so for Becky, because she was the one who had recommended the man to the committee for consideration. She and the other committee members knew that many of those who had voted against the man, as well as those voting for him, were truly seeking God's will. Wanting to point fingers at fellow church members, the committee could not. Though they did not understand why, they knew a spirit of confusion had gripped their church. One thought kept Becky from giving up completely on ministry or from growing bitter toward fellow believers: "An enemy has done this!" She knew that "God is not a God of confusion, but of peace" (1 Cor. 14:33 NAS). Not God, not people, but an unseen enemy had caused the confusion two pastor search committees could not seem to overcome.

### 3. Rest in the justice of God.

Over and over, the Bible teaches that those who plot the downfall of others will themselves fall. Haman, for example, plotted to have Esther's uncle, Mordecai, hanged. God intervened, however, and through decree of the king, Haman was hanged on the gallows he had prepared for Mordecai.

In dealing with spiritual enemies, you will not see God's justice meted out so quickly. You *will* see victories of God's people over Satan. You will see defeat of some of the devil's strategies. But God's Word states that the final fall of Satan and his demons will not happen until the end time.

In the meantime, rest in God's sure promises. Cling to them. Claim that "the wicked will fall by his own wickedness" (Prov. 11:5 NAS).

Cry out to a just God for the overthrow of the evil one. Pray David's prayer in Psalm 35 or other similar scriptural prayers against the spiritual enemies who have brought about your fall.

## 4. Purpose to get back up.

Someone who accidentally trips and falls may want to lie still awhile from embarrassment. But a person who's been tripped—and knows it—will tend to jump back up, even when really hurting. He or she will want to make clear that the "tripper" has not won.

Samson spent his final days in a Philistine prison blind, enslaved, degraded. His mistress Delilah and her Philistine cohorts had engineered his downfall. (His own lack of self-control put him within the enemy's reach.)

But regardless of the cost, Samson refused to stay down. When thousands of Philistines gathered to praise their god for defeating him, Samson prayed, took hold of the two middle columns holding up the building, and pushed with all his might. The structure collapsed, killing Samson himself and thousands of enemy Philistines.

The pastor search committee on which Becky served was astounded when the church voted not to call the man they had recommended. However, they took time to get their wind back and then began again to look for a pastor. They were determined Satan would not have the victory.

The second man they brought before the church was accepted by an almost unanimous vote.

As a Christian guided by the principles of the New Testament, you are under God's orders not to take revenge on persons who may have maliciously tripped you. Instead, look beyond those persons. There, you will find spirits whose sole intent is to destroy God's kingdom and replace it with their own.

Seeing them, you can gain new determination to stand again in God's power. You can learn to land blows that will stun and cripple your unseen adversaries. With confidence, you can declare: "Do not rejoice over me, O my enemy. Though I fall I will rise" (Mic. 7:8 NAS).

# 3

▼▼▼▼▼▼▼

# Glance Backward:
# The Sin Factor

As the doors of the state mental institution closed behind her, Theresa felt God had left her. She'd become a Christian at age 11. She knew her Lord would never forsake her. Still, it seemed He had. How else could she have been diagnosed schizophrenic? How else could she be in such a place?

She rose early each morning and tried to pray. One morning, an aide who found her kneeling beside her bed ordered her back into bed. Although another aide protested, "It's not going to hurt for her to pray," Theresa wondered if praying would help, either. She felt her cries were hitting the ceiling and bouncing back.

Each morning, she tried to read her Bible. She could not concentrate, though, because of the strong medication she was taking.

She read God's Word aloud to the other patients until she was ordered to stop. When she kept reading secretly to one bedridden woman who begged her to do so, the aide who caught her threatened to take away her Bible.

Three months after Theresa entered the hospital, one of her prayers was answered. She was released.

But going home proved to be a nightmare, too. Her unsaved husband treated her just as harshly as before she was hospitalized. Members of her church avoided her. For years she had served as church pianist and a Sunday School teacher. Now, others had taken over those tasks. Heavily sedated with tranquilizers, Theresa knew she could not have handled the positions, anyway. She still had trouble praying to God, and even thinking.

"My life was so miserable I begged the Lord to let me die," she remembers.

What had brought her to such a point?

At 19, Theresa had married a man she knew was not saved. "I felt I could change him after we were married," she says. She now knows that was foolish.

For years, she lived with his mental and physical abuse. She reared their three children. "Within a year after all our children left home, I became very depressed," she says.

She threw herself into a battle to keep liquor out of the area where she lived. "I spent many hours in research, writing legislators, speaking in churches and various groups concerning what the Bible says about this dreadful sin," she recalls.

Her home life continued to be turbulent. She confesses, "I had become so involved in my work that I wasn't eating right, sleeping well, or taking care of my body.

"We won the dry force battle against alcohol, but my 'fasting' and problems at home tumbled in on me. I was taken to the hospital and termed schizophrenic by a psychiatrist, given tranquilizers, and taken to the state mental institution."

A number of factors led to Theresa's mental fall. Some were beyond her control. But looking back at what happened, Theresa had to admit that her own sins helped bring about her failure. "I was not taking care of my body. I experienced carnal thoughts, bouts of pouting, resentment, and bitterness."

## FACING FACTS

Christians expect the ungodly to fail. Sometimes, we even reproach God because we do not see the wicked falling as quickly or decisively as we would like. However, we never expect to fail ourselves—even when we know we're not exactly toeing the line spiritually.

We never expect it—but it happens—because even in the lives of God's people, sin begets failure.

In Leviticus 26, God impressed on the nation Israel the importance of obedience. He said, "If you live according to my laws and obey my commands . . . You will be victorious over your enemies. If you will not obey my commands . . . You will run as if you were being pursued in battle, and you will fall when there is no enemy near you" (vv. 3, 7, 14b, 36b TEV).

Though the Israelites lived out the proof of these truths time after time, they never did learn consistency in obeying God. Consequently, they kept meeting defeat.

The apostle Paul said, "These things happened to them as examples and were written down as warnings for us. . . . So, if you think you are standing firm, be careful that you don't fall!" (1 Cor. 10:11-12 NIV).

## PRAYING FOR PERSPECTIVE

As you deal with failures in life, you will make no lasting progress until you are willing to analyze honestly the role your own sins have played in your fall.

Your sin may not be the dominant factor in a failure you have faced. But if any sin played even a small part in causing your defeat, it needs to be identified and forsaken.

## TAKING INVENTORY

What, then, are some wrong attitudes or actions that can lead to failure? Here are several to look for as you glance backward.

*1. Pride*

Amaziah, king of Judah, tried most of the time to do right in God's sight. During Amaziah's reign, God enabled him to win a great victory over the enemy Edomites.

Heady with his triumph, Amaziah decided to go to war against the Northern Kingdom of Israel. Israel's king, Jehoash, was not a godly man, but he sent Amaziah a wise warning: "You have defeated Edom, and now you've grown proud. Go ahead and congratulate yourself, but stay at home! Otherwise, you'll cause yourself and your country to fall."

The Bible says, "But Amaziah would not listen" (2 Kings 14:11 NAS). He went out to battle against Jehoash. His troops were defeated, and he was taken captive.

Those who have leadership roles in the church must take special care to guard against this sin. Pastors, teachers, and others in positions of responsibility may, at first, lean wholly on God for grace to carry out their tasks. Then, as they gain confidence in their work, they may shift their reliance from God to themselves. Before they know it, pride is born.

God's warning is clear: "Pride leads to destruction, and arrogance to downfall" (Prov. 16:18 TEV).

If you discover pride lurking in the shadows of your spirit, admit it to yourself and to God. In so doing, you will be humbling yourself before the One who opposes the proud but gives grace to the humble.

## 2. Stubbornness

Stubbornness goes hand-in-hand with pride. It's the mindset four-year-old Megan shows when she's told to brush her teeth or make her bed and she says, "I will not." It's the sin the Israelites committed when, standing at the edge of the land God had promised them, they balked.

Webster defines stubborn as "resolute; unyielding; obstinate; difficult to handle, manage, or treat." Does that sound like anyone you know? Perhaps, you could name persons who say (by their attitudes, if not their words), "Don't talk to us about what's right. Tell us what we want to hear. Let us keep our illusions. Get out of our way and stop blocking our path."

Would it surprise you to know that in Isaiah's time God's people said the same thing? Isaiah warned them that undealt-with stubbornness would lead to sudden ruin: "You are guilty. You are like a high wall with a crack running down it; suddenly you will collapse. You will be shattered like a clay pot, so badly broken that there is no piece big enough to pick up hot coals with or to dip water from a cistern" (Isa. 30:13-14 TEV).

Isaiah also gave the people God's remedy for stubbornness: repentance and quiet trust in Him.

If you have a stubborn streak, you will almost certainly not want to admit it. But by God's grace, you can. For your own good, you must.

## 3. Greed

Aesop told the story of a dog that found a bone. As the dog crossed a plank over a stream, he saw his reflection in the water. Thinking he was seeing another dog with a bone, he decided to get that bone, too. He snapped at his reflection—and lost his bone into the stream.

The Bible warns that those who want to get rich will be snared by foolish, harmful desires and sucked down to ruin and destruction (see 1 Tim. 6:9-10).

You may be gripped by the desire for more possessions, more prestige, more recognition, more control over others' lives. Any desire which keeps growing and refuses to be satisfied can be labeled greed.

If greed has you in its clutches, hurry to Christ. Give your desires over to Him. Then follow His step-by-step leading. He will teach you contentment. Don't be discouraged if the process takes time. One day, if you persevere, you will be able to say with the apostle Paul, "I have learned to be satisfied with what I have" (Phil. 4:11 TEV).

### 4. Sins of the tongue

When it comes to the tongue, the smallest of slips can sink the largest of ships.

Becky's church was at a crisis point. One pastor search committee had dissolved itself after a year of unsuccessful searching. The second committee had presented a man, only to have him voted down by the church.

Church members had been without a pastor a year and a half and were pressuring the committee to come up with a pastor, quickly. Becky and the five others on the committee were still in shock from the previous church vote. And now there was a rumor going around the church.

According to the rumor, the church's former pastor, Joe, had said a preacher named Mitch should be the next pastor.

The committee was considering Mitch, along with several other men. But more than one committee member had serious reservations about calling him. They simply did not have peace that he was the man for their church.

Pastor Joe had not written or called the committee to recommend Mitch for the position. Such a recommendation would have carried great weight, since members all believed Joe to be a man in close contact with God. But they didn't even know for sure what he had said.

Becky volunteered to call him. When she did, Pastor Joe told her, "I didn't say Mitch was *the* man for your church. I said he might be a good man for you. And I only said that to one person. I could recommend Mitch, but I could also recommend a dozen others."

Becky reported back to the committee. Now they knew the truth, but they were still in a dilemma. They could not bring Mitch before the church with integrity. They wondered: If we bring another man, will church members who have heard a misleading rumor and who place great weight on Pastor Joe's words vote our second prospective pastor out, too? Because of one misplaced remark, the search committee again stood on the brink of failure.

26

Have your words been true, pure, kind, and helpful? Have you spoken only what would please God and build up others? Or have you sunk your own ship with what you've said?

Solomon said, "He that hath a perverse tongue falleth into mischief" (Prov. 17:20 KJV). The words translated, "he that hath a perverse tongue," literally mean, "He that is turned in his tongue."

God wants to shoot your words straight and true, like arrows that always find the target. If your tongue has turned aside from the guidelines for right speech laid out in the Bible, admit to Christ that your mouth has been your undoing. Go with words of repentance to anyone you have offended. Ask the Holy Spirit to tame your tongue.

## 5. Immorality

"Adultery is a trap" (Prov. 22:14a TEV).

"He who is cursed of the Lord will fall into it" (Prov. 22:14b NAS).

In God's eyes, sexual sin is wrong. Whether those involved are married to other partners or unmarried, God cannot and will not condone their actions. He created sex to be experienced only in the bounds of marriage. He knows the grief that abused sexuality invariably causes. In fact, His Word says that a person who enters an immoral relationship is "like an ox going to the slaughter" or "a bird darting into a snare" (Prov. 7:22-23 NIV).

Moral sin can bring downfall in any area of life. More than one political candidate who was aboveboard in business and political dealings, but morally askew, has found his career ruined. Besides careers, moral sins can ruin health, effective parenting, friendships, decision-making skills, personal development, Christian witness, and, of course, marriages.

If you've toyed with or sped full throttle into immorality, run for your life! Run out of the path of temptation, out of the relationship that is dragging you down, and into the waiting arms of Jesus. He stands ready to forgive.

## 6. Injustice

We serve a just God. As Christians, we have been created anew in our Lord's image. We have His capacity for justice within us—yet we can still commit great injustice.

Parents can show favoritism to one child over another. Church members can silently reject fellow Christians whose social status, race, or education does not match their own. Persons in the work force can treat their employers, employees, or customers unfairly.

God's people can fail to take action against society's flagrant injustices.

Proverbs 28:18b says, "He whose ways are perverse will suddenly fall" (NIV).

If you have let injustice creep into your dealings at home, church, work, or play, approach the righteous Judge. He will lay your punishment on Jesus—if you will but plead guilty.

*7. Quarrels with fellow Christians*

"How wonderful it is, how pleasant, for God's people to live together in harmony!" (Psalm 133:1 TEV). How unpleasant it is for God's people to clash! Christians who wage war—even a cold war— with one another are headed for a fall.

In Paul's day, believers in the church at Corinth were quarreling and taking their quarrels to court. Paul soundly rebuked them for airing church disputes before heathen judges. He declared, "The very fact that you have legal disputes among yourselves shows that you have failed completely" (1 Cor. 6:7 TEV).

Have you let a quarrel with a fellow believer go unsettled? Are you harboring bitterness, anger, or resentment toward another member of God's family? Has your failure to love others led to other failures in your life or ministry?

God has given believers the capacity for unity with one another by His Spirit living within us. If that unity has been broken between you and another Christian, confess your part in the shattering. Ask the Lord to renew and sustain the oneness you've lost. Seek ways to heal the hurts.

If you and the other person are unable to restore the broken relationship yourselves, seek out a wise, Spirit-filled believer to help settle your dispute.

## INVITING INSPECTION

Sin that leads to a fall need not be flagrant. Theresa had opted to stay with an unsaved husband. She had served faithfully in her church. She had taken a stand on a moral issue in her community. None of those things could we call sin. Yet sin had crept in and remained, undealt with.

In Revelation 2, Jesus warned the Ephesian church that they were in a similar position. They had worked hard. They had shown great patience. They had taken a stand against evil men. They had suffered for Christ's sake and had not given up. "But this is what I have against you," Jesus declared, "You do not love me now as you did at first. Think how far you have fallen!" (vv. 4-5 TEV).

Most people would not call the attitude described above *sin*. But God does. He soundly rebukes those who serve Him with a half-hearted love.

Have unseen wrongs within weakened you—as termites weaken wood—to the point that, when the onslaught came, you could not stand? If so, God alone can point out those wrongs to you. He will not do so, though, until you invite Him to come for inspection.

## Joshua's Invitation

Joshua and the Israelites had just tasted their first victory in Canaan. They had watched the walls of Jericho fall, and, at God's command, had utterly destroyed everything in the city.

A few Israelite soldiers set out to conquer the tiny village of Ai. Instead of another victory, however, Israel suffered a sound defeat. The 3,000 men who made the attack were routed by the men of Ai. Thirty-six of Joshua's soldiers fell dead.

Throwing himself before the Lord, Joshua challenged God to tell him why such a defeat had happened. God answered bluntly, "Israel has sinned!" (Josh. 7:11 NIV). Someone had taken from Jericho items the Lord had told the Israelites to destroy.

God later pinpointed a man named Achan as the one who had done the wrong. Caught, Achan admitted he had stolen a beautiful robe, five pounds of silver, and a gold bar weighing over a pound. He had hidden his booty under his tent.

Joshua and all Israel took Achan to a place called the Valley of Trouble. There, the Israelites stoned and burned Achan, his family, his possessions, and the stolen items.

Then, at God's direction, all the soldiers of Israel went back to fight Ai. Some troops hid to the rear of the city. The rest approached Ai, as before. Again, the men of Ai came out to fight Israel. The Israelites appeared to flee.

But this time, when the men of Ai pursued the Israelites, the troops waiting in ambush came out of hiding and captured the city. They then surrounded the men of Ai and killed them all.

## God's Picture

The story of Achan and Ai paints a graphic picture for those today who think they can toy with sin. Israel overlooked one sin and suffered great military defeat. Likewise, one undealt-with area of sin in a Christian's life can lead to great spiritual defeat.

When Israel cooperated with God, they saw defeat turn to victory. Attacking Ai God's way, they destroyed their enemies. In fact, the men of Ai ran right into Israel's trap.

In your life, too, God can build victory, not merely in spite of defeat, but on defeat.

## Our Prerequisite

Sin slipped into the Israelite camp. Defeat came when sin was covered. Victory arrived after sin was exposed, confessed, and ruthlessly eradicated.

The Christian who wants to overcome failure must, like Joshua, be willing to hear when God says, "You have sinned!" She must allow her Lord to pinpoint hidden wrongs. She must cooperate with Him in ridding her life of them.

As she yields to Him, He will give her the desire and power to do the purging work He requires. "For it is God who is at work in you, both to will and to work for His good pleasure" (Phil. 2:13 NAS).

*When you're guilty*

In reading thus far, you may have uncovered a sin you had not labeled or faced before, yet you now realize contributed to your fall. Perhaps God has allowed you to fail, partly in order to bring that sin to your attention.

Name your sin to God. Offer no excuses. Express your commitment to forsake your wrong attitude or actions, by God's grace. Ask Him to forgive and cleanse you. Then, accept His forgiveness. With the load of guilt removed, you will soon be able to rise and walk again.

*When you're sin-hardened*

Furthermore, you may have recognized one or more sins that you knew were dragging you down, yet you refused to forsake. You may, in fact, have continued in certain sins so long that you no longer blush about them.

If you remain unashamed and unrepentant, God gives a stern warning: You will one day fall to your death (see Jer. 8:12; 10:15).

Can you blush now? If so, red face and all, lay down your most guarded sins. Deliberately turn away from them—and toward Him.

*When you're innocent*

Finally, you may have failed and yet be blameless. In looking back at the factors that led to your failure, you may find you have no sin to confess.

That doesn't mean, of course, that you are sinless. The Bible declares that every person does wrong (see Rom. 3:23; 1 John 1:10). You **do** sin. Yet, you may have failed—or appeared to have failed—innocently. You may find, after honest confrontation with God through prayer and Bible study, that He presents no sin to you to confess in connection with your failure.

The pastor search experience at Becky's church was like that. When church members voted not to call the prospective pastor the committee had recommended, all six committee members spent much time in desperate, seeking prayer. They realized they had missed what many of their people wanted in a pastor. They knew some things to do differently next time.

But God's Spirit did not convict any of them that sin had caused their failure. (They couldn't assume the problem was another's sin, either. Some very godly church members voted against the man they had recommended.)

If you believe you have failed innocently, make sure you give the Lord ample opportunity to tell you otherwise. Be willing to hear whatever He might say. Then, if He does not call specific wrongs to your mind, accept your innocence.

Your Lord will not plague you with the constant feeling that you must have done something wrong. Your enemy, the devil, will introduce that feeling. In addition, your own tendency to believe the blame must lie with you will keep you bound. If you let Satan and self have their way, you won't be able to get up again for fear that whatever unidentified wrong you did might unknowingly happen again.

When God declares you innocent, don't allow yourself to stay imprisoned by fear and guilt. Test the bars. Accept the fact that He has unlocked them, and walk free.

## GAINING VICTORY

Remember Theresa? The year after her release from a mental hospital was one of the most miserable of her life. Flat on her face, she believed she would never get up again.

But, she did. A Christian neighbor invited her to attend a weekly Bible class. In studying the Scriptures, she found healing for her mind.

She continued taking tranquilizers for some time. Then, God brought someone into her life who helped her gain victory over the pills.

She found bodily healing through healthy foods, vitamins and minerals, and other treatments prescribed by a doctor.

She stayed with her husband and continued to pray for his salvation. She nursed him through a four-year battle with cancer, and was present when, in the early-morning hours before his death, he prayed to receive Christ. Her marriage had lasted nearly 30 years.

Theresa, now in her 60s, works as a volunteer in a women's shelter sponsored by her denomination. "Many of the problems our ladies are facing, I have faced," she says.

"Little did I know [when I entered that hospital] that God would use my experience in the future to minister to many who have been placed in mental institutions and that I would be able to give warning to those headed in that direction."

Not all mental illness is caused by self-inflicted actions. Often, no reason can be found for why a person has become mentally ill. However, not taking care of ourselves physically, emotionally, and spiritually can lead to problems. Theresa recognized actions on her part that had contributed to her mental problems. She admitted and actively attacked these wrong actions. And God has built victory on defeat.

## POSTSCRIPT

When you find your nose in the dust, lift your head long enough to confront any sin lurking behind you. Allow Jesus' shed blood to erase it. Then, rejoice, declaring, "I may be in the dirt, but the dirt is no longer in me!"

That done, take a deep breath and gather your strength for yet another backward look.

# 4

▼▼▼▼▼▼▼

# Glance Backward:
# The Support Factor

Like Alice in Wonderland, Stephanie fell in a hole—and thought she would never hit bottom. The fall began when she was nine years old. That year, her beloved pastor father died of a heart attack.

Before his death, Stephanie's dad had been the hub in the wheel that kept her family going. Without him, Stephanie, her mother, and her brothers felt lost.

Stephanie's fall continued through her later childhood years. Overweight, she felt that the only one who had loved her and accepted her was gone. She began telling herself she would never be any good.

Sometimes, she still remembered that God had saved her at the age of six; the next year, He had impressed on her that He had a special purpose for her life. But most of the time, Stephanie listened to the negative thoughts she was telling herself.

By the time she reached seventh grade, her depression was so deep that she was "not even wanting to make it any more." She says, "I was always at church. I was a part of all the activities, but I would go home and feel empty."

During her teenage years, Stephanie did not outwardly rebel. She did not drink or run around with a bad crowd. But inwardly she did rebel, especially against her mother.

Some days, Stephanie expressed her anger and defiance by going into her room as soon as she got home from school and not coming out the rest of the evening. During those times, she did not speak or communicate at all with her mother, if she could help it. If forced to communicate, she said things designed to hurt.

"Many nights," she recalls, "I'd just cry and cry and cry. And I didn't even know what I was crying for."

During college and seminary studies, Stephanie pushed her feelings of anger and bitterness into a back corner of her heart. She enjoyed her seminary days. She was on her own for the first time in her life. She made friends. She supported herself with scholarships and by working two jobs.

She took great pride in the fact that she was making it without help from anyone. At times, the feelings of depression, inadequacy, and anger began to creep out of the corner where she had tucked them. But she pushed them down again, thinking, "Christians are not supposed to feel this way."

She says, "I had these erroneous ideas that one day I would wake up and be everything God wanted me to be, that all this unhappiness I'd felt, all this bitterness and anger would leave me, that all I had to do was get my seminary degree, get a job in the ministry, and everything would be wonderful."

Stephanie hit bottom late in her last year of seminary. She was about to graduate but had no job. She wanted a position helping hurting people in Jesus' name. She had believed for more than 15 years that this was what God wanted her to do. But nothing was opening up. She decided to stay full-time for a while in one of the jobs she'd had during seminary. But suddenly, funding for that job dried up. She had to give up her apartment and find a less expensive place to live.

One day, walking across campus, she felt empty and hopeless. She had fought long and hard not to let depression overtake her. That day she could not fight any more.

On reaching her apartment, she got out some antidepressants prescribed by a doctor and took what remained in the bottle. She thought, maybe this will end it all.

When she didn't die, Stephanie became scared. She was afraid that one day she might try again to commit suicide—and succeed.

A seminary professor helped Stephanie take her glance backward. After entering a pact with her in which she promised not to attempt suicide again, he led her to probe her past and to face her anger.

Soon, Stephanie graduated. She still didn't know what God wanted her to do. She didn't even feel He was there.

She took a summer job working with inner-city children, but she was miserable. One weekend, she visited her family. Seeing her deteriorated condition, her mother and brothers said, "You're coming home."

To Stephanie, coming home meant admitting defeat. It meant swallowing her pride and facing hidden hurts. It meant taking the risk that God might leave her in her small hometown forever. Initially, she thought, "I can't do that." But she did.

To give some order and purpose to her life, she began looking for a job locally. For four, then five, then six weeks, she walked the streets. She says, "It took every effort I had to get up out of bed each day."

Finally, she was offered a minimum-wage job. She prayed, "Lord, don't You have something better for me? I don't want to do this." But she took the job. She tried to do her best at it.

During those weeks at home, Stephanie came to terms with herself and her anger. She began to accept and love her mother. In fact, her mother became her best friend.

At the same time, the Lord became very real to Stephanie. She says, "God became my Father."

A month-and-a-half later, Stephanie was offered the job she'd been longing for. She moved to another state to become director of a Christian shelter for women.

Some women who come to the shelter are battered; some are divorced and jobless; some are prison parolees; some, alcoholics or drug addicts. Almost all are at the bottom of a long fall. Stephanie is able to tell each of them, "I fell, too. But Jesus Christ helped me. He brought me up out of the pit. And He can do the same for you."

## WHAT HAVE YOU BEEN LEANING ON?

You're down. You want to know why. It's time to glance backward again, to see what—or whom—you've been leaning on. Both lack of support and a false support can lead to a fall.

## NO SUPPORT

Anna, a high school student, walked out the glass doors of the brick school building one February day. An ice storm had started not long before, and school officials were dismissing classes early. Already, the sidewalks were slick.

Trying to take the steps carefully, Anna thought, "Wouldn't it be funny if I fell?" Then, suddenly, she fell. It wasn't funny.

Anna thought she was being careful. She believed she had things under control. But she fell because the situation was more than she could handle—and she had no support.

Stephanie's fall, too, came about in part because of lack of support. At nine years old, she faced a tragic loss. Yet, somewhere along the way, she had developed the attitude: "I can handle it myself."

She didn't feel she could draw comfort from other family members. She didn't allow fellow church members or friends to see how badly she was hurting. She went to great lengths in college and seminary to be financially and emotionally self-sufficient.

Certainly, every person needs to "carry his own load." Galatians 6:5 states just that. But the same chapter gives a balancing command: "Help carry one another's burdens" (v. 2 TEV).

Joab and Abishai were brothers. Both were commanders in King David's army. One day, Joab led David's army out to battle. Ready to attack a certain city, he discovered enemy troops both in front of and behind his men.

Joab carried his own load. He took a band of choice soldiers and prepared to lead them to attack the Aramean troops coming up from the rear. But Joab also let someone else help carry his burden. He put his brother Abishai in command of the rest of the Israelite soldiers. He told Abishai to attack the Ammonites to the front.

Joab said to his brother, "If the Arameans are too strong for me, then you are to rescue me; but if the Ammonites are too strong for you, then I will rescue you. Be strong and let us fight bravely. . . . The Lord will do what is good in his sight" (1 Chron. 19:12-13 NIV).

Like Joab and Stephanie, we need the support of others. Above all, we need the support of God.

## Relying on Self Rather Than on Jesus

Jesus said, "You can do nothing without me" (John 15:5 TEV). He didn't say, "nothing except . . ." If someone were to ask, "Are you relying on Jesus?" could you say yes? Might you say yes, and not realize that you have, in truth, been self-reliant?

Below are some danger signs that can indicate a failure to throw one's full weight on Christ. If you've recently "fallen," ask yourself: Did any of these attitudes characterize my life before my fall? Even if you've not encountered failure lately, ask: Do any of these qualities characterize me now?

The key word in both questions is *characterize*. Every Christian will occasionally find herself guilty of one or more of these attitudes. However, if any of them appears often in a person's life, it may signal a dangerous self-reliance that can lead to a fall.

## 1. Worry

God's Word commands, "Don't worry about anything" (Phil. 4:6 TEV). The same verse explains what to do instead: Go to God, admitting your need; be specific; as you pray, thank Him for what He's already done and will do to answer your prayers.

If you have given all your needs, decisions, and problems over to Christ, if you are standing on the truth that He is in control and that He will work everything together for good for His people, then He promises you will have peace. A person simply cannot rest in Christ and worry at the same time.

When the pressure's on, does your stomach churn? Do you have tension headaches? Do you walk around with a high-blood-pressure blush in your cheeks? In these and other ways, your body may be telling you that you have not accepted the strong support God gives.

## 2. Presumption

How do you start each day? How do you make the decisions each hour brings?

Presumption heads in a direction that seems good, without taking into account God's leading. Presumption is the bedfellow of common sense. "'For My thoughts are not your thoughts, neither are your ways My ways,' declares the Lord" (Isa. 55:8 NAS).

God will give you wisdom to make decisions, but only as you make sure you are lining up your will and your thoughts with His. That requires daily time spent with Him. It requires asking, "What is Your will?" regarding major decisions and seeking His answer in His Word. It means not hesitating to ask Him about minor decisions, either.

Often, God will give you freedom to make routine or split-second decisions without conscious prayer. But to make those choices wisely, you must have a listening heart. You must be ready, at His Spirit's prodding, to stop or change courses.

Presumption ignores the tug of God's Spirit. It walks through doors God has closed.

If you've been presumptuous, you may have experienced the truth of Proverbs 14:12: "There is a way which seems right to a man, but its end is the way of death" (NAS).

### 3. Frustration and anger

How do you react when you run into problems beyond your control? The one who relies on God will consciously roll the weight of these problems over on the Lord, knowing they are His responsibility. The one who is self-reliant may well pitch a fit.

June, from chapter 1, experienced great frustration and anger when the Arab students in her English classes did not cooperate. The more she tried to correct the problem, the more frustrated and angry she became.

She says, "I kept thinking I could do it. I could meet the situation. I could finally get the material right." She now knows, "I should have been relying more on God, not on myself."

You cannot make your spouse stop drinking or your children more obedient. You cannot make your boss recognize and appreciate you. You may not be able to control where you live or whether you marry or how much money you make. But that's OK, if your life is in the hands of the blessed Controller of all things.

If you find yourself easily angered and chronically frustrated by the things in life beyond your control, you may be trying to live your life without His support.

### 4. Confusion

"God is not a God of confusion but of peace" (1 Cor. 14:33 NAS). Where He is in control, order reigns.

If confusion characterizes your life, could it be that you're trying to do it your way?

### 5. Pretense

Many Christians put on Sunday smiles, along with Sunday clothes, and walk into church acting as if everything is fine, when it's not. Maybe, like Stephanie, they think that's the way they're supposed to act.

The person leaning hard on God, however, isn't afraid to let others know she's leaning. She lets God make her life transparent. She doesn't try to protect her reputation. She knows that showing her weaknesses frees God to show His strength.

## Refusing to Let Others Help Shoulder the Load

Do you take seriously the "one anothers" of the Bible? You know: "love one another," "serve one another," "encourage one another," "comfort one another," "confess your sins to one another," "pray for one another," "bear one another's burdens."

Do you let God weave other Christians into the fabric of your life? Or, do you try to go it alone and, thus, reject the support system your Lord has created for you?

God sometimes allows burdens on us that He intends others to help carry. How can another believer help bear your burdens, though, if you are hiding or clutching them?

In her book, *My Ducks Are Really Swans*, Deanna Harrison tells about a time she failed as a teacher. She had signed on to teach a high school resource class, supposedly for students with mild learning disabilities. She soon learned the class was also a last resort for incorrigible troublemakers.

Two of those troublemakers declared war on Deanna. Determined to teach the two as well as her other students, Deanna emerged from each class physically exhausted and emotionally bruised. Equally determined to see their young teacher fail, the two youth disrupted every class session. Toward the end of the term, they also began to threaten to "get" Deanna after school hours.

Two days before the school year ended, she resigned.

Deanna believes she went down in that battle because she did not call out for reinforcements. Through the whole year, she says, she did not tell anyone what she was experiencing. She tried to handle it alone.[1]

Of course, if you let others know your deep needs, you risk their unconcern or rejection. If you seek others' counsel, you risk hearing what you don't want to hear. Still, God has made us "members of one another" (Eph. 4:25*b* NAS). Those who have taken the risks have found: He works through His people's interaction.

In Chapter 11, you will learn guidelines for letting others share your burdens. For now, however, decide whether you, like Deanna, have met defeat because you failed to cry, "Help!"

You'll have to humble yourself to admit you need support from the Lord, as well as from others. Perhaps, in God's plan, that's the whole point.

## FALSE SUPPORTS

Just as dangerous as life without support is trust in the wrong support.

Anita's dad had just hung her new porch swing. He sat down in it. She sat next to him. Suddenly, one end of the swing crashed to the floor, taking them with it. She hurt her ankle as well as her dignity.

Her dad had not attached the swing to a stud.

Have you leaned on any of the following false supports, only to have them give way? Are you dangerously close to a fall because of too great a reliance on someone or something?

## People

Jim was walking to class across a snow-covered college campus. A girl he was passing slipped and fell on the slick sidewalk. He offered his arm to help her up. Just as she got her balance, he fell, pulling her down again. Jim had great intentions, but no better footing than the one he was trying to help.

God does want Christians to rely on one another—as long as we build our mutual support on the foundation of trust in Him. Those who look to others *instead of* to God for their support are on dangerous ground. They are acting like the Israelites who, when threatened by Assyria, ran to Egypt rather than to the Lord for help.

God pronounced woe on those Israelites. He warned, "He who helps will stumble, he who is helped will fall" (Isa. 31:3 NIV).

You can get into trouble by resting your life on the advice or philosophies of:

❑ *worldly "experts."* They know nothing, and want to know nothing, of God's ways. Like the Pharisees of Jesus' day, they are "blind guides." Those who follow them are also blind. "And if a blind man guides a blind man, both will fall into a pit" (Matt. 15:14 NAS).

❑ *psychics, astrologers, and others flaunting "New Age" methods of guidance.* What people today hail as new, God condemned ages ago (see Isa. 8:19-20). He detests occult practices (see Deut. 18:9-12). He will not be worshiped by persons who give Him lip service, but dabble or step outright into the things of Satan.

❑ *"yes-men."* These include employees, coworkers, or "friends" who tell you what you want to hear. Ahab, king of Israel, died because his "yes-men" encouraged him to attack a certain city. Before leaving for the battlefield, he threw into prison the one man who had courage to say, "You will be killed if you go." Yes-men may give you a sense of confidence, but it will be a false one.

❑ *well-meaning people who wrongly believe they have a word from God for you.* Advice from others, even from Christians solidly committed to God, must be filtered through God's Word and your prayers before being acted on.

Wanda wanted a baby, but had been unable to conceive. One day, Amy phoned to say, "I have a message from God for you." Amy then read Wanda a Scripture about resting in the Lord. Then Amy said, "If you want a child, you must lay down all the activities you are doing and just rest."

Earlier that week, God had reminded Wanda of the very Scripture Amy had read. But Wanda had not felt that God was telling her to quit everything she was doing. Confused, she prayed about the matter for days. Finally, Wanda decided that God had, indeed, impressed a Scripture verse for her on Amy's mind, but that Amy's interpretation had been her own. Wanda continued to obey what she believed God had told her to do. Within a year, she became pregnant.

You can also get into trouble by seeking to draw strength from:

❏ *persons unable or unwilling to meet your needs.* When people who know about your struggles seem unconcerned or overwhelmed by problems of their own, don't get upset with them. But don't try to lean on them, either.

❏ *persons who have proven untrustworthy in the past.* Somewhere along the way, you will probably lean on someone you believe to be a trusted friend—and find you've been betrayed. You can't avoid that, unless you refuse to trust anyone. But you can beware of trusting someone who has a habit of making promises and failing to keep them. Like Charlie Brown, you will land flat if you keep trying to kick footballs you have let the Lucys in your life hold.

❏ *persons you have put on a pedestal.* Before leaning on anyone, make sure both of you are standing on level ground. Why? When your life is interwoven with another Christian's, you can't help but see each other's weaknesses. Be prepared for the missteps and falls of even the strongest Christian. Otherwise, disappointment with a person you greatly admire may cause you to lose your own footing.

## Material Things

Many people try to build their lives on "things." As Christians, we may shake our heads over the materialism in our country and not realize how materialistic we ourselves are, unless something happens to wake us up.

Perhaps you were used to a certain standard of living—and then you got married, or divorced, or lost your job. Suddenly the props were knocked out. You had rested more weight than you knew on "things." Perhaps you've been making your life decisions based on what will bring you the most profit financially. God warns: "Those who depend on their wealth will fall like the leaves of autumn" (Prov. 11:28 TEV).

## Your Own Security Blanket

Isaiah declared, "Woe to those who . . . rely on horses, and trust in chariots because they are many, and in horsemen because they are very strong, but they do not look to the Holy One of Israel, nor seek the Lord!" (Isa. 31:1 NAS).

You probably aren't relying on chariots or horses for success. Why not take those two words out of the above verse and then fill in the blanks with your own?

What have you always expected to come through for you? Have you relied on education or a certain job? Have you trusted in your expectations for your children? Have you looked to banks or other institutions for your protection?

Security blankets may make a child feel safe. However, they don't make him any safer than he already is. And they can occasionally trip him up. Spiritual security blankets will trip you up, too.

## RE-ESTABLISHING SUPPORT

If you've been leaning on any false support, or if you've been trying to be your own sole support, have the courage to admit it. Otherwise, you will only hurt yourself.

Then, take these three steps:

*1. Recognize that what you leaned on simply was not strong enough to support your weight.*
Don't try to place blame. Simply face facts.

*2. Let go.*
Let go of any bitterness and resentment you may be carrying toward whoever or whatever failed you.

*3. Turn your face in a new direction.*
If you've taken seriously the backward glance of the last two chapters, you've had to be painfully honest with yourself. That's good. It's a first step toward recovery.

But it's only a first step. If you keep looking back, you will never get up and go on.

Stephanie says, "I deal with women all the time [who] are so tied up with hurts of the past, things that have happened to them, whether they're imagined or unimagined, that they cannot live another today or tomorrow."

Don't be like those women. Instead, say with the apostle Paul, "Forgetting what lies behind and reaching forward to what lies ahead, I press on" (Phil. 3:13*b* -14*a* NAS).

---

# 5

▼▼▼▼▼▼▼

# Glance Backward:
# But I Didn't Fail

Stunned, William sat in the home he would soon have to vacate. He was a pastor. That is, until today he had been a pastor. During the morning worship service, his congregation had voted him out.

William tried to think through the situation, but feelings kept crowding out rational thoughts. Angry with himself, he wondered, "Why did I allow this to happen? Why was I so stupid not to see it and do something about it?"

Angry with church members who had just ousted him, he questioned, "How can they do this? I've spent six-and-a-half years ministering to them, marrying them, burying them, crying with them, laughing with them. How can they just decide they don't want me anymore?"

Angry with God, William cried out in his spirit, "God, listen. Here I am, trying to promote revival, which is what You say You would like to see happen in the lives of people, and then this happens. God, why did You do this?"

At moments when the anger subsided, William wondered what in the world he was going to do. He'd been in the pastorate 12 years. Now he had no church, no income, no home, no place to go. "What church will take a pastor who's been asked to leave another church?" he asked himself. "And even if someone will take me, do I want to go back into the ministry? Do I want to ask for this again?"

He was humiliated. He knew he would soon have to walk out his door and face people, especially fellow pastors. He knew what kind of reception he'd get. He had seen what happened when others lost their churches. Probably no one would say anything to his face, but preachers who knew him would whisper about him and keep their distance.

William wondered, "Why is it that, when other ministers say what I've said, God blesses them; [but] when I try to teach the same principles, I lose my church? I must be inferior. I must not be doing it right."

Then he would think, "No. I know what I've taught is true. I know what I've done is right."

He thought through the years he had spent at Crossroads Church, a small congregation in a Southern town. The church had averaged more than 30 additions a year. Baptisms and missions giving had increased steadily. Many new young couples, eager to serve the Lord, had joined. A youth ministry and a bus ministry had been established.

The growth and excitement in the church had come about, in part, because of growth and new excitement in William's life. While at Crossroads, he had been introduced to the Spirit-filled life. Though he knew God's Spirit had indwelled him since salvation, William now experienced the joy of giving the Spirit full control.

He wanted the church he pastored to know that same joy. He began to train church members to walk in the Spirit, witness, and pray. He began to preach often on the Spirit-filled life—sometimes to the exclusion of other important subjects.

He didn't see until it was too late that he had tried to move his people too far too fast. He didn't realize he had focused on one truth so much that his teaching had become unbalanced. In his excitement over the good things happening at Crossroads, he did not recognize the growing unrest among some longtime members. Those members not only had "never done it this way before," but also had always wielded the power in the church. They felt church control was slipping through their fingers.

New members were now holding church leadership positions. Worship services included strange, new elements like testimonies, choruses, and praise times.

The last straw came when William invited a certain preacher to hold a revival at the church. This preacher had an open and free style of praise and worship. William says, "The church was not ready for that."

Within weeks, he was no longer pastor.

As he sat in his home, hurt and broken, God sent the first ray of hope of recovery. The three-member staff of Trinity, a nearby church, drove up. They told William, "Hey, we're here, and we're supporting you. If we can help, just let us know."

Soon, other people began reaching out to William and his family. A member of Crossroads who did not agree with the church's decision provided a rental house free of charge. Other Crossroads members pooled their money and bought their former pastor needed appliances.

A Christian grocer offered William a job in his store. William took the job. He and his family joined Trinity Church. There, fellow Christians ministered to them and William had opportunities to minister to others. Though many fellow pastors reacted as he'd expected, a few expressed confidence in him by calling on him for pulpit supply.

For 10 months, William worked in the grocery, prayed, read his Bible, struggled with agonizing feelings and questions, and waited. Then, God opened the door for him to pastor again. At the same time, the Lord gave both William and his wife a promise from Psalm 23 that He would restore their souls.

## PARENTHESIS

Are you still looking backward, puzzled? Perhaps, while reading the preceding chapters, you have thought and prayed through what has happened to you. You've been as honest as you know how to be. Yet, even though people are pointing their fingers, shaking their heads, and feeling sorry for you, something inside you is saying, "But I didn't fail."

Perhaps God has put that conviction in your heart.

If it looks to all the world as if you've failed—but you haven't—you're in good company. Those who watched Jesus die believed He had failed, also. He'd said He was king, but now even His own disciples didn't see how He would ever rule anyone. However, they did not know about resurrection power.

Others who look at you—and even you yourself—don't know everything that is happening in your life, either. People judge by appearances, and appearances may well be wrong.

You may not have "produced" in a ministry or a job as others think you should. You may have made a decision that appeared to lead to disaster. You may have reared a child who forsook his or her Christian heritage.

Whatever the circumstances, you do not have to believe you have failed just because it seems you have. If you have allowed God to pass judgment on your attitudes and actions, His "Well done!" is all that counts.

Sometimes, though, discovering your "failure" was not a failure only adds to your hurt and confusion. You want to vindicate yourself, but who will believe you? You're torn between asserting, "I didn't fail," and thinking, "I must have failed." You feel trampled by a stampeding crowd. Not sure how you got down, you don't think you'll ever get up.

At those times, remember the One who went before you. He did not give up because of the cross! Consider what your Lord Jesus went through, and how He responded, so you may not become discouraged and give up (see Heb. 12:2-3).

### 1. He was silent before others.

Jesus' captors marveled at His silence. When accused, mocked, and beaten, He said nothing.

If you've been branded a failure, your first reaction may be to clear your name. You may be tempted to tell everyone who was really at fault.

Jeremiah, a prophet who knew from experience what it meant to appear to have failed, gave this advice: "When we suffer, we should sit alone in silent patience; we should bow in submission, for there may still be hope. Though beaten and insulted, we should accept it all" (Lam. 3:28-30 TEV).

Impossible, you say? Yes, it is impossible, if you want to cling to any shred of pride. To remain silent at such times is to humble yourself. As you choose to do so, God promises to provide you the courage and self-control you need to follow through.

Being silent means you do not announce to the world your side of the story. It does not mean you tell no one of your hurt and confusion. In Gethsemane, Jesus expressed His great grief and inner conflict to three chosen followers. You, too, would do well to find a few "significant others" to support you through your time of struggle.

Jan, the missionary forced to resign her Latin American field, talked with a seminary professor in the United States when Latin Christians treated her badly. Members of the pastor search committee on which Becky served talked and cried with one another when their search efforts fell apart.

If you have the opportunity to "present your case" before one person or several, do so in a way that protects Jesus' reputation above your own and that builds up His church. Do not do anything to bring division to His Body.

## 2. He cried out to God.

"My God, my God, why have you forsaken me?" (Matt. 27:46b NIV). Jesus had carried out His mission, just as planned. He knew His apparent failure would end in triumph. Yet, in the midst of His death struggle, He did not hesitate to admit His human feelings to His Father.

You, too, can freely express hurt, anger, and confusion to God. William suggests that you not only speak your feelings to the Lord, but also write them down. Keep a journal of your pilgrimage through seeming failure. He says, "You'll look back later, and God will use what you've written to minister to your heart and to show you where you've been."

As you cry out, remember:

❑ *Jesus' cry showed He had immersed Himself in God's Word.* His question, "My God, my God, why have you forsaken me?" is the first line of Psalm 22. That's no coincidence. Many times in His ministry, Jesus showed His familiarity with the Old Testament Scriptures. As a dying man, with no strength for speeches, He used that one question to express to believers of all time the intense, conflicting feelings He was experiencing. To know something of what went on emotionally while our Lord was dying physically, all we must do is read the rest of Psalm 22.

To keep from bitter ravings, your cries, too, must be built on time spent in God's Word. Under the weight of your confusion and hurt, you may not feel like hurrying to the Word. More likely, you will not feel like opening it at all. But regardless of your feelings, discipline yourself to read the Bible daily. It is your lifeline. No matter how tired or disillusioned you may become, do not let it go.

❑ *Jesus' cry went unanswered.* Our Lord asked why. At other times in Jesus' earthly ministry, God the Father had spoken to Him audibly. This time, the Father made no response.

Like Jesus and countless others, you may ask why. That's OK. It's also OK to want God to answer. But don't let your faith in Him go to pieces if He doesn't.

❑ *Jesus' cry of confusion was followed by a cry of faith.* "Father, into your hands I commit my spirit" (Luke 23:46 NIV). Christ began by calling His Father *God* and asking *why*. He ended by calling God *Father* and entrusting Himself to Him.

Once you have vented your distress to God, praise Him. More than likely, you will not feel like praising. Still, offer Him the sacrifice of praise. Worship Him as your holy, sovereign, and loving Father. Climb into His arms as a hurting child seeks comfort from an earthly father. Entrust yourself, your reputation, and your future to Him. (Chapter 7 covers the roles of Bible study, prayer, and praise in recovery more indepth.)

God's Word promises that if you will commit your way to the Lord and trust in Him, "He will make your righteousness shine like the dawn, the justice of your cause like the noonday sun" (Psalm 37:6 NIV).

*3. He forgave those who were at fault.*

He cried, "Father, forgive them!" (Luke 23:34). You can, too. Here again, you'll have to make a choice that will probably go against your feelings. You'll have to decide as an act of your will that the score is settled.

Forgiving does not mean you won't remember what happened. It means you no longer remember with animosity. It means you no longer count the incident an offense. (Chapter 10 discusses forgiveness more fully.)

Unlike Jesus, you may also need to seek forgiveness for wrongs you have done. Even if you did not fail, wrong attitudes or actions on your part may have added to a troubled situation. William, for example, recognized that pride and lack of balance in his teaching contributed to his forced resignation. Wrong attitudes or actions may also have slipped in *after* your apparent failure. You may, for instance, have allowed bitterness to take root and grow.

To those dealing with apparent failures, William advises, "Be honest with yourself. Do not assume that everybody who's accused you and everybody who has said something about you is wrong in every area. Have enough initiative and courage to say, `Listen, I may be wrong.' Face yourself squarely and say to God, `I want to come out of this situation closer to You and more conformed to the image of Your Son.'"

*4. He looked to the future with joy.*

Jesus endured Calvary, the ultimate apparent failure, "for the joy set before Him" (Heb. 12:2 NAS).

Does it seem you have failed, when you haven't? Are you being trampled by your own feelings of hurt, anger, and confusion, as well as by others' beliefs that you've blown it? If so, join with those who must admit, "I've failed," and take the steps to recovery outlined in the rest of this book.

In the meantime, while things still look unspeakably bleak, don't give up hope. Keep believing that, on the other side of the hurt, you will again find joy.

An elderly Christian was once asked his favorite Bible verse. He replied that his favorite Scripture portion was not a whole verse, but a phrase that appears in the Bible many times.

"And that is?" the questioner asked.

"'And it came to pass,'" the elderly man replied.

Seeing the other person's puzzled expression, he continued, "Don't you see? It didn't come to stay. It came to pass."[1]

Rejoice, hurting one! What you're going through will pass.

## PERSPECTIVE

Roger Youderian, Nate Saint, Jim Elliot, Ed McCully, and Pete Fleming were murdered on January 8, 1956, while trying to carry the good news of Jesus Christ to Ecuador's Auca Indians. To the world, it looked like the five missionaries' mission had failed.

Weeks earlier, Roger had agreed to take part in the venture. But for days he struggled with the decision, not because he was afraid and not because he felt the undertaking a mistake. He struggled because he already felt he had failed as a missionary.

He had recently written in his diary. "About ready to call it quits. . . . I believe that the Lord chose the Jivaria [an Indian territory in Ecuador] for us but I just didn't measure up to it. You will say that when the Lord calls, He supplies. You can have my boots anytime you want them. It isn't there. I'm not good at pretending."[2]

Roger did not want to go on the Auca mission feeling God had left him. He did not want to be the weak link in the chain. So he prayed until he got God's perspective. And he found God's viewpoint 180 degrees from his own. He went out to his death—and to glory—expectantly, joyfully.

Did Roger blow it? Did he and the other four men meet defeat that January day? If so, the inspired writer of Hebrews 11 must have made a mistake, also. After lauding a host of unnamed saints who "conquered kingdoms" and won other great victories through faith in God, the writer then commended a group of believers we might consider losers: those who stepped out in faith and, as a result, lost their wealth, suffered embarrassment and pain, or were mistreated or killed. God's assessment is not, "They blew it," but, "The world blew it." Hebrews 11:38 states, "The world was not worthy of them" (NIV).

Three verses later, the writer makes his point: "Therefore, since *we* are surrounded by such a great cloud of witnesses, let *us* throw off everything that hinders and the sin that so easily entangles, and let *us* run with perseverance the race marked out for *us*" (Heb. 12:1 NIV, italics added).

When you're down, it may seem you will never run again. Do not give up. For, unlike Jesus and the five martyred missionaries, "in your struggle against sin you have not yet had to resist to the point of being killed" (Heb. 12:4 TEV).

Even if one day you do walk into death for Christ, you will not have failed. And everyone who counts will know it.

[1]*Guideposts Magazine.* Reprinted by permission from Guideposts Associates, Inc. Carmel, NY 10512.
[2]Elisabeth Elliot, *Through Gates of Splendor* (Wheaton, Illinois: Tyndale House Publishers, 1956) pp. 151-155, 195-196. Used by permission of Tyndale House Publishers, Inc. All rights reserved.

# 6

▼▼▼▼▼▼▼

# Gaze Upward:
# God Never Fails

Grant woke suddenly. Beside him, his wife, Ruth, roused too. It was 2:00 A.M. Two men stood in the couple's second-floor bedroom shining flashlights into Grant's face. One held a long knife. The other held a machine gun, pointed at Grant.

Grant was terrified. But he couldn't say he hadn't been warned.

He and Ruth were missionaries serving in a country characterized by unrest and violence. They had lived in that land more than 20 years.

Although conditions had always been unsettled in the area, things had recently worsened. "There was a total breakdown of law and order. Different neighborhoods were controlled by groups of armed men," Grant reports.

Grant was a school principal. The couple lived on a mission compound that included the school, a three-story building containing their apartment, and a large parking lot. Cars of missionaries who had left the country and a few who had elected to stay were parked in the lot. Among those vehicles were two vans.

Earlier, a neighbor had told Grant, "I think you ought to know, the gangs are stealing vans like the ones you have in the parking lot. They like to get hold of vans because it makes moving their men and arms from place to place quite easy."

Grant thanked his neighbor, but dismissed the warning. He thought, "We've been in this city a long time. We teach the children of the neighborhood. People know we're not mixed up in politics."

Later, one of the unarmed watchmen who guarded the school property at night told Grant, "Armed men have come into the school yard on several nights. They've demanded that I give them the keys to the building. But I have not given them the keys."

Another night, Grant and Ruth heard people prowling around the building in which they lived. A missionary staying on the ground floor saw one of the men. When she shined her flashlight in his direction, he ran away.

Amazingly, Grant still wasn't alarmed. The ground floor windows of the building were barred. The door was made of iron. He did not believe anyone could get in.

He did believe the reassurances of a friend who had children in the school and who, Grant now realizes, sometimes bragged too much. Himself a member of an armed gang, the friend had assured Grant, "We drive around the neighborhood at night looking after things. Don't worry. We are watching your house."

Ultimately, Grant simply believed God would protect him and his wife, as He had done in past years, without Grant taking any precautions. He was caught completely off guard when the two armed men managed to get up on a balcony, cut through a screen, and enter his home.

He says, "I cannot describe all that took place that night." He and Ruth were terrorized and humiliated. Grant was taken downstairs, where about eight other men waited. He was forced to unlock the garage and front gate of the mission parking lot.

The men left Grant and Ruth alive, but they took five cars and vans. They also took other valuables, including Grant's wedding ring and a watch Ruth had given him for his birthday.

Afterward, the couple felt degraded, betrayed, and shocked. Grant wrestled with great guilt. He explains, "I felt I had failed. I had failed to protect my wife. I had failed to protect the property entrusted to me. I had failed to heed advice of people who knew what was happening."

Though he knew others had been killed trying to resist during such raids, he wondered if he should have offered some physical resistance.

Time passed, yet the couple continued to suffer. Great wounds had been opened in their spirits and emotions. It seemed those wounds would never heal.

Among missionaries and believers in the area, Grant and Ruth were the first to be hurt in the conflict. They wondered, "Is God punishing us? Is our commitment to Him faulty?"

Grant and Ruth attended church meetings, only to hear others stand up and testify, "Shells have landed all around our house—and not one pane of glass has been broken." "We were in a car stopped by armed men—and we did not lose a single bit of money." "We were taken by armed people—and then released unharmed."

Over and over, believers declared, "God takes care of His people."

"Why didn't He take care of us?" the couple wondered. "What is His part in all this?"

Then, slowly, the healing began. First, the two returned to the states to take care of a family matter. There, they received encouragement and support from mission board leaders.

Ruth stayed in the US for a while to attend to a medical problem. Grant returned alone to the missions field. He went because he felt he had to carry on his work. However, he returned afraid. Fighting and shelling were still going on in the area. Armed groups still controlled the neighborhoods.

The situation had gotten so bad that all shops and businesses in the area closed. As a result, the men of the church Grant attended met daily for prayer, sharing, and sometimes a brief sermon.

Even though statements made in church meetings had, earlier, seemed only to deepen the wounds, Grant continued to meet with his fellow believers. He also spent much time reading his Bible and praying on his own. He says, "During those days, the Bible became very real."

God pointed him to the promises of Isaiah, reminding him, "But they that wait upon the Lord shall renew their strength; they shall mount up with wings as eagles; they shall run, and not be weary; and they shall walk, and not faint" (40:31 KJV).

On his bookshelf, Grant found an old book by E. Stanley Jones titled *Victorious Living*. He began to work through that book. God used its message, as well as prayer, fellowship, and Bible promises, to do His healing work in Grant.

## LOOKING UP FROM THE BOTTOM

It's hard to look up when you're lying prostrate. Sometimes, it seems impossible. If confusion, hurt, and anger are pummeling you without mercy, you may be very tempted, when you do look up, to shake your fist.

Suddenly, God is not the God you thought you knew, and you're not sure why. Is the situation too big for Him to handle? Has He made promises He can't keep? Has He gone to sleep or turned His back on you at your moment of greatest need?

However impossible the task may seem, your job now is to lift your head. As you do, raise your voice if you must, but not your fist.

The God you thought you knew is past knowing. You will never, with confidence, be able to predict what He is going to do in any given situation. You will never know anything of Him that He does not choose to reveal to you.

Yet, He invites you to know Him better. He offers to reveal Himself, if you will seek Him (see Jer. 29:12-14). Sometimes, when He seems the most hidden or the farthest removed, He is preparing to show you more of Himself than you have ever seen.

Let your situation prompt you to turn toward Him. Seek Him now.

## GOD OF UNSPOILED VICTORY

King David marched out to fight the Arameans, who lived north of Judah. While David was distracted, the Edomites attacked his country from the south. They inflicted serious damage, not only on his troops, but also on his land.

David was stunned. He was championing God's cause, yet God had let him fall before an enemy. Turning his face upward, David cried: "You have rejected us, O God, and burst forth upon us; you have been angry—now restore us!" (Psalm 60:1 NIV).

David did not understand why the God who could have prevented his defeat had not done so. Still, he recognized his Lord as the only One who could turn defeat into victory. He called on God to do just that. He claimed, "With God we will gain the victory, and he will trample down our enemies" (Psalm 60:12 NIV).

Our God is the God of victory. He cannot be defeated. Though His battles involve life-and-death matters, infinitely more vital than any game, His "winning streak" can be compared to that of a football team with an unbroken record of wins. He knows no losses, no ties.

He is the ultimate defensive strategist. When His enemies attack, He already knows both what tactics they will use and how He will respond. Always, His response is correct.

Primarily, though, His moves are offensive. In football, a good defense can keep a team from losing; but only rarely can the best defense, without an offense, win a game.

Before the world began, the Father took the offensive against sin and Satan when He planned Christ's coming. While on earth, Jesus promised, "My church will storm hell's gates victoriously" (see Matt. 16:18). The book of Revelation describes God's final offensive strategy and worldwide victory.

When you're down, you may not see a shred of evidence of God's triumph. Your own life may be in shambles. Your career or ministry may appear ruined. Your family may be torn apart. The world situation may seem to prove the God of love has somehow been beaten.

"I have overcome the world" (John 16:33 NAS), said Jesus on the way to Gethsemane. How ironic, how impossible that statement must have seemed to the disciples the next day as they watched their Saviour die on the cross.

Like those disciples, you have a choice to make. You can believe what, from all appearances, seems true. Or you can continue to believe that God is who He says He is: the God of victory.

Perhaps you can agree, "He is victorious," yet you feel He is no longer on your side. You may find yourself wondering, and even asking, "God, why are You fighting against me?"

In Psalm 60, David asked the same question. Yet, he clung to the knowledge that he and his people were God's people. He knew the key question was not, "Is God on my side?" but, "Am I on His?" Even in questioning, David kept believing his Lord would, again, show Himself strong in his behalf.

The same Bible that says, "He does not fail" (Zeph. 3:5 NAS), also promises those who belong to God: "He will not fail *you*" (Deut. 4:31 NAS, italics added).

If you have received Jesus Christ as your Lord, He is your strong defense. Even if He has allowed Satan's forces to break through and tackle you, you can know He has already planned for your recovery. Even now He is taking the offensive in your behalf.

In the upper room, knowing Peter would soon fall, Jesus said, "I have prayed for you, Simon, that your faith may not fail" (Luke 22:32 NIV). Today, Jesus is interceding for you. He is standing before the Father, pleading for your ultimate victory.

You can, of course, choose to reject the Lord because He has apparently rejected you. Or you can do as David did: Cry out to God. Express your distress. Yet, choose to cling to Him, confident He will enable you to triumph.

## GOD OF UNBROKEN PROMISES

Maybe, like Jeremiah, your crisis comes at the point of believing God's word.

Jeremiah was in the stocks. The wooden frame into which his feet, hands, and neck were fastened held him in a bent position. His back, a bloody mess, proclaimed the 40 lashes he had received. Men were mocking him, laughing at his torment.

His crime? Speaking God's message.

Years earlier, God had called Jeremiah to be His spokesman. At that time, the Lord promised Jeremiah: "They will fight against you but will not overcome you, for I am with you and will rescue you" (Jer. 1:19 NIV). Another day, God had repeated that promise to Jeremiah (see Jer. 15:20-21).

God's prophet had stepped out on God's promise. He had spoken God's message—and, now, the bottom had fallen out. It seemed God had forsaken His word altogether. Jeremiah cried, "O Lord, you deceived me, and I was deceived" (Jer. 20:7 NIV).

Like David, Jeremiah took his distress directly to God. He told the Lord what appeared to him to be true. Then, like David, Jeremiah moved from accusing God to praising God and stating his trust in Him (see Jer. 20:11-13).

The prophet didn't end his prayer on a note of praise, however. Rather, he spent five verses cursing the day he was born. Definitely still down, he had just begun to look up.

Psalm 12:6 affirms, "The promises of the Lord can be trusted" (TEV). It may appear to you, as it did to Jeremiah, that that statement simply is not true.

Maybe you claimed a promise from God for a lost or backslidden family member. Maybe you launched a ministry, got married, or entered a business deal based on a Scripture that spoke God's go-ahead to you. Maybe you claimed a verse promising you victory over a certain problem or habit. Whatever the promise, you stepped out on it, believing God had given it, and you fell flat. Besides feeling, "I've failed," you may also be thinking, "God has failed. He gave me this promise, and then He pulled the rug out from under me."

What do you do? Do you stop believing God? Before you begin to rant at Him, take time to consider other explanations for what has happened.

❏ *Have you "taken" a promise God did not give?* Second Corinthians 1:20 says all God's promises are "yes" in Jesus. All are available to God's children in Christ. However, not all can be claimed the way you may want to claim them in a certain situation. When God speaks a promise to you, His Spirit will stir within you in response to His Word.

❑ *Have you received a promise from God, but interpreted it incorrectly?* While you are accusing God of failing you, He may be at work fulfilling His promise in a different way than you expect.

❑ *Might God have different timing for fulfilling His word?* Before He brings His promise to pass, He may allow you to go through a time when what He has said will happen seems impossible.

God may have yet another reason for apparently failing to keep His promise to you, a reason known only to Him. The one explanation that is always wrong is that He failed. God is no liar. He will do what He says.

You may choose to stop building your life on His rock-solid promises. But if you do, you'll only have one place left on which to build—the sand.

You may choose to stop wielding His Word as the sword of the Spirit. But if you do, you will have thrown down your main means of spiritual attack.

Satan knows this. He knows that the word of God, handled properly, is our ultimate offensive weapon in spiritual battles. That's why, from the days of the Garden of Eden, he has been trying to get God's people to reject what God has said.

Like Jeremiah, you may find yourself speaking words of trust one minute and words of despair the next. But if you stop speaking those words of trust, only despair will be left.

## GOD OF UNFAILING LOVE

Matt, a campus minister, sadly said his goodbyes. Then he did what he believed he had to do: he left behind a six-year ministry at the university.

Relocating many miles away, he found it hard not to look back. He felt he had left his work at the university unfinished. Not that he hadn't done good work there. Indeed, his ministry had been complex, fruitful, and thrilling. Through outreach Bible studies, Matt had reached 20 to 30 non-Christian students a semester with the gospel. About a third of each semester's study group had become believers.

Matt had also led or supervised Bible studies for new Christians, as well as evangelistic training courses, and a discipleship course for mature Christians.

Now, he had dropped it all. Since there was no money for anyone to take over the work, he'd simply had to let it go.

And the work had stopped.

During the semester after Matt left, however, God tapped some

Christian students and a few university faculty members on the shoulder. They felt His tap, and responded.

Before long, they restarted the campus outreach Bible studies. Then, they implemented a follow-up Bible study, a discipleship course, and evangelistic training.

Matt left the university thinking his work had failed and fallen apart. Now he says, "It's succeeding in ways I never even conceived of."

God could have intervened to enable Matt to stay at the university, but He didn't. He let the crisis happen. He let the work stop. Then, He moved in to show His love and glory.

Jesus let another crisis happen not long before His death. He let his friend Lazarus die. Mary and Martha wondered if Jesus' love for them and their brother had failed. It had not. Jesus waited, and then moved in to raise Lazarus from the dead—*because* of His unfailing love for the three.

In the same way, Christ's words to you, His intervention on your behalf, even His refusal to intervene at times when you think He should, are built on His love for you.

The Bible affirms, "God is love" (1 John 4:8 KJV). He, by nature, offers deep and constant love to persons entirely unworthy of it. The Bible also declares, "Love never fails" (1 Cor. 13:8 NAS).

Even when in Old Testament times God's people failed again and again to obey Him or heed His warnings, He said, "I will not take my love from him" (Psalm 89:33 NIV).

God's great, undying love for His children is what makes His inability to fail a comfort, rather than a threat. If you knew Him only as a God who never suffers a defeat and never breaks a promise, you would stagger under the weight of your responsibility to live up to His standards. But remembering His love, you can run to Him with your failures, like a bruised child to a father, and find comfort and encouragement in His everlasting arms.

How long has it been since you sang "Jesus Loves Me?" How long since you considered the truth of those words?

Why not sing that chorus aloud now? If others are around, sneak off to a place where you can be alone for a few minutes. Or, sing right where you are, reminding those within earshot that Jesus loves them, too.

Think through the words as you sing them. Receive them into your soul and spirit. Then, choose to believe in God's unfailing love for you, regardless.

# 7

▼▼▼▼▼▼▼

# Gaze Upward:
# Invite Intimacy

Sara felt betrayed. She and Johnny had married three years earlier, with the understanding that they would one day have children. Both were Christians and the two had a strong marriage. Yet Johnny had just told Sara, "I don't believe God wants us to have any children."

Stunned, Sara wanted to yell at Johnny, "How dare you change your mind about this now!" She wanted to yell at God, "How dare you lead me into this marriage—and leave me childless!"

Each day after Johnny's announcement, Sara moved further away from her Lord and her husband. She read her Bible but found no comfort. She prayed but heard no answers. She and Johnny rarely talked. Times of intimacy became almost nonexistent. In fact, when Johnny tried to touch Sara, she felt repulsed or cried uncontrollably. Although the two put up a front for others, their relationship teetered precariously on the brink of ruin. Then, one day, through a Christian friend, God brought Sara up short. "Are you going to divorce Johnny?" the friend asked.

"No," Sara answered, almost surprising herself. "I vowed to stay with him for life; and I'm going to stay."

"And you'll choose to enjoy life with him, even without children?"

Sara paused. Finally, she answered, "Yes."

Sara's friend then offered her some valuable advice. "Start looking for ways to show Johnny you love him. Invest treasure in him, even when you don't feel like it."

Sara followed her friend's advice. She wrote Johnny love notes. She bought him "happies," little gifts to bring him cheer. She cooked his favorite dishes. She began to turn toward him, rather than away from him, when he desired intimacy. To her surprise, her attitudes soon began catching up with her actions. She found her love for him rekindled. She found her desire for him revived.

Nearly four years later, Sara gave birth to the couple's first child. She had not coerced or manipulated her husband. On his own Johnny came to believe, "God does want us to have children."

## LOST INTIMACY

Have you felt betrayed by God, as Sara felt betrayed by Johnny? If so, your intimacy with your Lord has almost certainly suffered.

Have you made the same choice Sara did: to stay with the One to Whom you've committed your life? If so, be aware that you may not feel closer to the Lord immediately. You may feel numb. You may still want to withdraw when He tries to touch you.

Will you, then, take the next crucial step in your recovery process? Will you deliberately turn toward your Lord, rather than away from Him? Will you focus on recapturing intimacy with Him?

Twice in Solomon's Song of Songs, the beloved woman realized the one she loved had left! Did she simply assume he would return and busy herself doing other things? No, she went out searching for him. Even when the search lasted all night, she did not stop. When night watchmen who came upon her beat her and took away her cloak, she didn't quit crying out for her loved one.

Both times, the woman's search was rewarded. She and her lover were reunited; their intimacy restored.

You, too, can recapture intimacy with your Lord. If you miss the closeness you once shared, begin to seek desperately the One Who loves you. Choose to invest treasure in your Bridegroom.

## PATTY: INVESTING TREASURE

Patty kissed her son Justin good night on Christmas night 1978, and turned to leave the room. Four-year-old Justin began to cry. When Patty turned back to find out what was wrong, Justin said, "Daddy's never coming back, is he?"

Justin's daddy, Philip, had walked out that day, after seven stormy years of marriage to Patty. The couple had not told their son the situation. Yet, he knew.

Brokenhearted for her child, Patty also hurt for herself and her broken relationship with Philip. The two had married young, after dating only four months. Patty later learned that Philip had a drinking problem. She also discovered that his drinking life-style and her church-going one did not mesh.

Eight times in seven years, the couple had separated. Each time, Patty had been the one to walk out. Now she was left behind. And this time, the separation was permanent. Philip had found someone else.

The week between Christmas and New Year's, Patty cried a lot. She did not think she could live without her husband. She also did a lot of soul-searching. She felt she could have done more to make her marriage work.

On New Year's Day, when all the bills were due, Patty suddenly realized she had the same bills she'd always had—and only half the income. She dropped down on her knees and began to pray.

Admitting to God that she could not do it by herself, she asked for His help. She turned all her finances over to Him, promising she would give Him a tenth of every penny she got. (She and Philip had tithed sporadically during their marriage.) She told the Lord she was trusting Him to look after her.

When Patty later sat down and tried to figure out how she would make ends meet, she says, "There was just no way on paper that I had enough money to pay the bills." As each bill came due, however, she paid it. Every month, the Lord supplied the needed money.

During the year of separation before her divorce, Patty stayed active in church. She served as church pianist. She took a leadership role in the single adult department.

After the divorce, Philip, who by then had moved to another state, came to pick up Justin for his first weekend visit. Patty cried from the time Justin left until Philip brought him back three days later. She says, "I really felt like I was never going to see my child again."

For a whole month, Patty agonized over the approaching weekend when her son would leave once more. The weekend came. Justin left with Philip. This time, Patty turned again to the Lord. "OK, Lord, I trusted you with my money, and You've not let me down. Now, I'm trusting You with my son. He's in Your hands, Lord. I trust You to take care of him and to bring him back to me safely."

That weekend, instead of sitting home crying, Patty got out of the house and went shopping. She says, "Since that visit, I haven't cried or been upset when my son [has] left." On occasions when she would feel the tears starting to come, she would say, "Lord, take over. Justin's Your child."

Patty soon began to believe God had a special task for her to do. After praying and seeking her pastor's advice, she volunteered to spend a month establishing a ministry to single adults in an area of the US with few evangelical Christian churches. Doing such a ministry meant, among other things, leaving Justin for the month.

Still trusting God, Patty accepted the challenge. She now says of the days before and during that trip, "That was probably the time in my life when I felt the closest to the Lord."

When God allowed divorce to happen in her life, Patty may have felt like turning away from Him. Instead, she chose to turn toward Him—to offer Him her finances, to trust Him with her son, and to obey His call to risk. Now remarried to a Christian, she is continuing to invest treasure in the One who stayed with her and kept loving her even when a human relationship failed.

## YOU: CULTIVATING CLOSENESS

You invest treasure in someone by entrusting him or her with something valuable to you. Investing treasure is an act of the will. A person invests money not by feeling like it might be a good thing to do, but by doing it. You invest treasure by taking action. You invest treasure by taking risks.

In financial investments, you will often get the biggest returns by putting away a small amount of money regularly. In the same way, you will reap the most benefits from "treasure investing" when you determine to make it a consistent, ongoing project.

Investing treasure in God will deepen your relationship with Him. Why? Because "where your treasure is, there will your heart be also" (Matt. 6:21 NAS). Begin today taking steps that will turn your heart back toward Him.

*1. Spend time alone with Him.*

One thing precious to everyone is time. One thing necessary to build relationships is time. Invest time in your Lord daily. Spend time seeking Him in His Word, crying out to Him in prayer, adoring Him in praise and thanksgiving.

Sara read her Bible daily during the long months when despair seemed to have a stranglehold on her. Much of that time, she could see nothing there for her. God was silent. The words were just words on a page. She felt no quickening of the Spirit to let her know that any of those words held special meaning for her.

Still, Sara sensed that to stop going to God's Word would be to let go of her lifeline. She kept reading.

One day, she saw a glimmer of light. She was reading Isaiah 50:10-11. There she found this insight: Sometimes God's servants—even those who reverence and obey Him—will walk in darkness. She found this command: Don't try to light your own fire; trust in the Lord; rely on your God.

She continued to go to God's Word. Finally, after months of clinging to her lifeline, Sara began at last to feel that the Lord was indeed pulling her out of the mire into which she had fallen.

Jan, in chapter 2, reached a point in the midst of deep depression where she could not pray. For months while serving as a missionary she tried to cry out to God, but words would not come.

The first Sunday after her return to the US on medical leave, Jan heard this sermon illustration:

> A grieving woman had gone to her pastor, distressed, because she could not pray. The woman told the minister, "All I can ever get out is, `Oh, God—' I can't get past that."
>
> The pastor replied, "That's when the Holy Spirit takes over and prays for you." Then he quoted Romans 8:26: "The Spirit also helps our weakness; for we do not know how to pray as we should, but the Spirit Himself intercedes for us with groanings too deep for words" (NAS).

Hearing that story, Jan felt a great weight being lifted off her shoulders. She says, "I knew God was with me. I knew He was doing things in my life. But I was having trouble reaching out to Him. Then, to realize that the Spirit was there reaching back and forth and holding us together, that was very, very beautiful to me."

If you find Bible reading and prayer tough to do when you're flat on your face, how much more impossible may praise and thanksgiving seem. Praising God when you are angry with Him may, in fact, seem like hypocrisy. Yet, when everything in you cries out against thanking God and speaking well of Him, you have the perfect opportunity to offer Him the *sacrifice* of praise—praise that costs you something.

Praise offered when you feel happy and in control may be easy—

and cheap. Praise given because you choose to do so, even when your feelings refuse to cooperate, is costly. It is a treasure invested.

If you're willing to spend time reading your Bible, praying, and praising—but you're at a loss as to how to go about it—try reading systematically through the Psalms. Read aloud to the Lord passages that express both your heartcry and your confession of who God is and what He's done. Offer Him the treasure of time spent with Him, even when it seems He is not there.

### 2. *Spend time among His people.*

Remember that Christ's church is His Body. Time spent with His people is time invested in Him.

Grant's home had been raided by an armed band (chapter 6). At first, Grant gained no comfort from mingling with God's people. Other Christians' testimonies of God's care only made his and his wife's situation seem more unbearable.

Still, Grant persisted in meeting with fellow believers. God used those times of fellowship to help heal Grant's deep hurts.

Grant urges, "If failure does come, don't leave the church. **There**, is your strength; and **there**, are people who care, who pray for you. Some of them will understand; some will not. But stay with the church. Worship. Praise God. Be with His people."

### 3. *Seek ways to please Him.*

Delight in doing little things—or big things—to make your Lord happy. That, of course, entails finding out what makes Him happy through study of His Word. It involves obeying in faith what you believe His will is. Such acts of obedience may take a million different forms.

While separated from her husband, Patty remembered that tithing pleases God. She began to tithe. Later, she realized God wanted her to tackle a new ministry. Again, she obeyed.

You might delight God by seeking forgiveness from someone you have wronged or by doing a kindness to someone who has wronged you. You might cultivate new, godly attitudes. You might renew a Christian discipline you had laid aside. You might get your finances in line with the principles of God's Word. You might begin a program of Scripture memorization, or speak out about God's goodness to non-Christians as well as to Christians.

If you cannot hear God's voice giving you specific guidance right now, find a scriptural principle you know He wants His people to live by. Then, live by that principle.

Say, for example, your husband or wife has children by a former marriage. As much as you love your spouse, you've failed to make your blended family work. Yet God says, "Love one another." You study the qualities of godly love in 1 Corinthians 13. You choose, by God's grace, to spend yourself in behalf of your spouse's children. You don't do it to please them. You don't even do it to please your spouse. You do it to please God.

Seek to bring God pleasure in ways that seem tiny or insignificant. Haven't others' tiny acts of thoughtfulness delighted you?

Seek to please God in ways that seem impossibly big for you to handle. What better way to express your faith in Him?

### 4. Demonstrate your trust in Him.

You will be able to do things pleasing to God only if you let Him do something for you: take over.

Imagine yourself in an airplane cockpit on a taxiway, preparing for takeoff. You've never had a flying lesson, but you've watched a pilot friend a few times. The weather is calm and clear. You think you can handle it.

Suddenly you see your friend knocking frantically on your window. You open the door of the plane. Over the roar of the engine, you hear him saying, "You're crazy. You can't do this. Let me take you up."

You remember the last time you went up with him. He flew into some bad weather, and you got sick.

So what will you do? Will you trust him to fly you to your destination, even though you feel he let you down once before? Or will you decide, "No, you let me down; now I'm going to handle this myself."

Even if you're uneasy about it, move over and let God take control of every aspect of your life—especially those areas you most want to grasp. Otherwise, you will be heading for a crisis far greater than any you have experienced in the past. As you give God the controls of your life, He will prove Himself able to get you where you need to go.

Patty gave her finances over to God. Only then was she able to tithe as she knew God wanted her to tithe. She entrusted her son into God's keeping. Only then was she able to leave Justin for a month to minister to others in Jesus' name.

Asa, king of Judah, had spent his whole monarchy trying to please God. He had led his people to destroy their idols and worship the

Lord alone. As a result, God had given Asa a reign of peace.

One day, however, an Ethiopian commander named Zerah marched against Judah with an army of one million men. Amazingly, Asa did not panic. He did not complain, "Lord, why are You allowing this to happen?"

Instead, he mustered an army about half as large as Zerah's and took up his battle position. Then, Asa prayed: "Lord, there is no one like you to help the powerless against the mighty. Help us, O Lord our God, for we rely on you, and in your name we have come against this vast army. O Lord, you are our God; do not let man prevail against you" (2 Chron. 14:11 NIV).

When Asa demonstrated his trust in God, the Lord enabled Asa's army to crush the invading troops. After the battle, God sent a prophet to give Asa a personal message of encouragement. That message was, for Asa, a love letter from his God. It sparked Asa to intensify his spiritual reforms in Judah. It led to a whole nation knowing new intimacy with God.

## GOD: WELCOMING ONENESS

Are you seeking the Lord eagerly, desperately? Are you:

- ❏ spending time alone with Him?
- ❏ spending time among His people?
- ❏ seeking ways to please Him?
- ❏ demonstrating your trust in Him?

Re-establishing lost intimacy is never easy. But when you're seeking to draw closer to your God, you have one big advantage: the One toward Whom you are reaching wants oneness even more than you do.

His silence and His seeming absence do not mean He has rejected you. Perhaps, He is increasing your desire for Him.

If you will make a practice of investing treasure in the One Who has apparently abandoned you, you will one day find His heart and yours again beating as one.

# 8

▼▼▼▼▼▼▼

# Look Inward:
# Test Yourself

Don's fall shocked everyone. Almost everyone, that is. Don had grown up in a church-going family. When he was about 11 years old, he walked the aisle and was baptized. As a young adult, he quit church for several years. Then, he and his wife, Caroline, and their two sons joined a church and became active members.

Don attended Sunday School, sang in the choir, and coached the church's softball team. His oldest son accepted God's call to enter into a church vocation. Life appeared to be fine.

But all the while, Don was digging a pit. And one day, he fell into it.

His digging tools? Greed and alcohol. During Don's childhood years, his church-going family was poor. They lived in constant turmoil. Don grew up with two desires: to get away and to have money.

He joined the Air Force at 17. After a four-year stint, he married, signed up for a second term in the service, and had two children, before finally settling down to civilian life. Meanwhile, Don's hunger for money grew. He developed a beer drinking habit that also grew until it controlled him and created turmoil in his home.

After working for a finance company for several years, Don jumped at a chance to get into insurance adjusting. "I knew all the ways a man could make money in that business," he says. "I could buy and sell junk and still draw my salary. I'd be out in the public, where I could find wrecked cars, houses, boats, airplanes, or anything else I wanted and sell them and make a profit on them."

The more money Don made, the more he wanted. Before long, he found he couldn't satisfy his greed by honest means; so he turned to dishonesty. For example, he would pay more to a repairman than it cost to fix a damaged vehicle. He and the repairman would split the profit.

Then, he says, "even that wasn't enough. My greed just took over my life." Don rented a lockbox and set a goal. "If I can get $100,000 in hundred dollar bills in that lockbox, I'll quit and start going straight," he told himself.

He never did get that $100,000. What he made, he spent.

The more Don became involved in fraud and stealing, the more problems he had in his marriage. He and his wife, Caroline, a Christian, weren't getting along at all. Don says, "I knew if I was going to continue to steal I couldn't do it and live with her. So I just left." He walked out on Caroline and their two sons, one of whom was now in college, the other in his senior year of high school.

Not long afterward, Don got caught. He was asked to resign his job. Knowing the FBI was investigating him, he sold everything and moved to another state. He took with him Eva, a young woman whom he married.

Eva encouraged Don to go to church with her. The first Sunday the couple attended services together, God's Spirit confronted Don. Realizing he had not been saved as an 11-year-old boy, Don surrendered his life to the Lord. He and Eva also joined the church that morning. He did not know at the time all that surrender meant, but he did know he needed to try to live without sin and to cultivate a one-on-one relationship with God.

Ten months later, Don was indicted on 17 counts of mail fraud. He was tried, convicted on two counts (the other 15 were dropped), and sentenced to five years in a federal prison.

During his trial, Don told the truth about his illegal dealings. He says, "I had surrendered to the Lord, and I wasn't going to lie." When sentenced, he traveled alone 400 miles to the prison and turned himself in. He walked into prison four years and three months after walking out on his first wife.

Four months later, while Don was praying and meditating one night, the Lord convicted him of his need to ask forgiveness of the family members he had hurt so badly. Unable to sleep, he got up in the wee hours of the morning and wrote Caroline, his two sons, and his mother and sisters. He told them he had become a Christian. He asked their forgiveness for hurting them so deeply.

Don had begun his climb out of the pit.

## TAKING THE TEST

Have you ever failed a test? John thought he had flunked a big one. He had taken the written exam to get his private pilot's license. Then, he received a letter saying he had scored only 66 on the test. He needed a 70 to pass.

John was devastated. He had his heart set on flying. Surely, the score was wrong! He had checked his answers after the test and thought he knew which ones he had missed. Besides, when he added up the missed questions on the score sheet, they didn't equal the printed total. Frantic, he called the Federal Aviation Administration to see if someone there had made a mistake.

The FAA hadn't made a mistake. Some friends of John's had sent him a counterfeit test result. When he thought he'd failed, he had really passed.

John's story had a happy ending. But what if John's friends had counterfeited a passing grade when John had really failed? His devastation would have been worse—and longer lived.

Our enemy, the devil, has a similar trick up his sleeve. He loves to make people think they are "passing" spiritually, when they are not.

In Norway, for example, 97 percent of the people belong to the state church. However, only 3 percent attend services regularly. Most Norwegians think church affiliation is enough to make them right with God. Are they right?

The apostle Paul said, "Test yourselves to see if you are in the faith; examine yourselves! Or do you not recognize this about yourselves, that Jesus Christ is in you—unless indeed you fail the test?" (2 Cor. 13:5 NAS).

The test Paul wrote about—the test to learn where you stand in relation to God—is the most crucial test you will ever take. What better time than now to take it? Maybe God has allowed you, like Don, to face a failure in some area of life so He can show you a more urgent failure you need to correct. Or, maybe you need reassurance that, regardless of what failures you may meet, you have passed the one test that matters.

To take this test, you will have to look inward. You will not be able to base the results on appearances. Church-going choir member Don appeared saved, especially to those outside his immediate family, but he was not.

Have you ever had strep throat? It rears its ugly head regularly

69

among the children in our town. One child with strep may have a headache, an upset stomach, and a terribly sore throat. Another child with the same germ may show no symptoms. Still another may have symptoms similar to strep—but not have strep.

You cannot test for strep throat by observing the symptoms. The only way to know if you have it is to undergo a throat culture. Likewise, you cannot test yourself spiritually by noting whether you go to church, pray, read your Bible, and live morally right. To know where you stand in God's sight, you must let God reach down inside you with the swab of His Word. You must accept what the Word reveals about your spiritual status.

You've looked back. You've looked up. Now, gather your courage, and look inward. Mentally mark your answers to the following questions. Test not the strength of your relationship with God but the reality of it. The rest of your life, the rest of your eternity, hinges on what you find.

*1. Have you ever considered yourself wicked?*

If your answer is yes, you're on the right track. If no, please reconsider.

God's Word says every person who has ever lived, except Jesus Christ, has been wicked from birth. Of course, some appear more wicked than others. And no matter what evil a person has done, she will consider herself as "pretty good." Except, perhaps, when she's down.

That's why, if you've had a fall, now may be a good time for an honest assessment.

Have you ever seen yourself as wicked? God has. His Word says (Write your name on the blank lines):

_____ has turned away from God;
_____ has gone wrong;
_____ does not do what is right;
_____ has sinned and is far away from God's saving presence (author's paraphrase based on Rom. 3:12, 23 TEV).

Are you offended? Ask God to show you what you naturally are. When He does, you'll be undone.

That's why you can't base a passing or failing grade with God on how good you or others think you to be. *No one* is good enough to "make it" in God's eyes. He is like a teacher who requires a score of "perfect behavior" every moment of every day to pass His course. He notes every wrong attitude, wrong motive, and wrong word or deed. And you are human, imperfect, and prone to do evil.

God doesn't set such an impossible standard out of meanness. He does it, in part, to protect heaven from taint. One sin, committed by Adam and Eve, corrupted and devastated our entire world. If heaven is to be free from tears, suffering, sorrow, and dying, it must be utterly sin-free.

Amazingly enough, then, the first step toward making a passing grade with God is to admit, "I've failed. Lord, I cannot live up to Your standards." It's a simple step, but often a very difficult one. To take it means to turn your back on your pride.

Judy had been baptized twice. Now a young adult, she went to her older sister one day, crying. Judy knew she was still not saved. Wanting to go to heaven, she had done what she felt she was supposed to do to get there. But having been "good" all her life, she'd not wanted to admit, "I'm wicked. I'm not nearly good *enough* by God's standards."

That afternoon, in her sister's den, Judy cried out to God, "I deserve hell. Lord Jesus, please save me!"

### 2. Do you understand the end of the wicked?

Proverbs 11:5 says, "The wicked will fall by his own wickedness" (NAS). Remember now, "the wicked" includes not only murderers and rapists; it also includes you. Unless God intervenes, you will bring about your own downfall.

Apart from Christ, you may fall in a way that wreaks havoc in your life and the lives of those around you. Apart from Christ, you will ultimately fall in an infinitely more devastating way.

One day, death will come. For those who have trusted in anything other than the saving power of Jesus Christ, death will mean a sudden plunge into a black, burning abyss. No one gets up after that fall. It is irreversible. Its unspeakable pain lasts forever.

### 3. Do you know the provision of Christ?

What a horrible dilemma! All are failing a test that means the difference between life and death. All are running headlong toward the edge of a cliff, with no power to stop themselves.

What a relief to learn that God in His grace and mercy provided the solution even before man created the problem. God planned before the world began to send Jesus Christ. Jesus, in His great love for us, came to earth as a baby, grew up without sin, and gave His life on a Roman cross in our behalf. By the death-shattering power of God, Jesus rose on the third day. One day, He will return to earth to separate those who have passed God's ultimate test from those who have failed (see Acts 10:38-43).

In effect, Jesus Christ laid Himself across the abyss into which every person would have fallen. All who choose to step out on Him are saved from that horrible fall. As they walk along from day to day, they find sure footing, constant provision, and undergirding strength. Even when they stumble, they have the power of Christ Himself to help them get up and go on again.

Many, however, have chosen not to accept Jesus' provision for them. Instead of stepping out on Him, they have tried to step around Him. As a result, He has become to them, not a rock on which to walk, but a stone over which to stumble. Matthew 21:44 warns: "And he who falls on this stone [Jesus] will be broken to pieces" (NAS).

Did you realize Jesus had made such a provision for you? If so, have you pondered lately the depth of love it took for Him to provide you life?

*4. Have you thrown the full weight of your eternal destiny on Jesus Christ?*

Don had fallen into his own pit; he could not get out. One Sunday morning, he saw Jesus as his only hope. Don was still down. He was alienated from his family and on the road to prison. But, admitting his failure, he crawled to the only One who could save him. In that instant, he moved from failing to passing God's test.

Knowing about Jesus can only take you so far. Receiving the life He offers requires making a choice. You must admit your desperate need for the Saviour. You must trust that His sacrifice alone is enough to put you right with God. You must choose to lay down your life in order to take up His.

If you have taken this step, rejoice! No matter how many and how hard the falls you experience, "underneath are the everlasting arms" (Deut. 33:27 NAS). If you have not committed your life to Christ and received Him as your Lord, why not do so now?

You can pray, in these or your own words, "Lord Jesus, I see my wickedness. I confess it. I know I cannot be inwardly clean and right with God by my own doing. You are the only way to God. You are God. You died and rose again for me. Please save me."

## ACCEPTING YOUR SCORE

If you have just prayed to receive Christ, or if you have ever prayed to receive Christ, you're new! God the Holy Spirit now lives in you!

Does that mean you will never fall again? No, it means that whatever falls you take, you can know they are not fatal. Whatever failures you may face, you can know you have passed the ultimate test

# 9

▼▼▼▼▼▼

# Look Inward:
# Accept Yourself

Caroline drove into her driveway, stepped out of the car, and walked back to the street to pick up her mail. It was October 1987—her birthday, and the day of her mother's funeral.

Caroline was alone. Her former husband Don had left her four-and-a-half years earlier. He had since remarried. Caroline's two sons were now grown and married themselves.

She opened her mailbox and found a letter from Don. He was writing from prison—not knowing her mother had died, not realizing the letter would arrive on her birthday—to tell her he had become a Christian and to ask her forgiveness.

Caroline had prayed for Don's salvation many times since the day he had left her. Having received Christ as a 10-year-old, she'd assumed through most of her married years that her husband was also saved. When she became aware of Don's dealings, though, she realized he did not know the Lord.

After Don left, Caroline had also prayed about her own situation as a single-again. Bewildered and distraught at being abandoned, she focused at first on all the wrongs Don had done to her. Then, slowly, she began to see the wrongs she had done.

❑ She had stayed a baby Christian. Most of her teenage and adult years, she'd attended church regularly, but had not grown in the Lord.

❑ She had been so emotionally tied to her husband she had not left room for God to be God in her life.

❏ She had lived in self-will. Thinking she had the strength to "fix everything," she had tried to do just that.

❏ Even before separation and divorce, she'd been bitter, resentful, and miserable. Slowly, she came to understand why she had been so unhappy. "I was one of the Lord's, and I wasn't living like it. I was following many of my husband's ways and was miserable in doing it," she says.

Through the crisis of divorce, Caroline began changing into the person God had intended her to be all along. As she immersed herself in Bible study and sought the prayers, counsel, and fellowship of other Christians, God began changing her.

She realized she could not fix her marriage or her ex-husband's life. Releasing both to the Lord, she experienced joy, even in sadness. She found a peace she had not previously had.

She answered Don's letter soon after receiving it. "Yes, I forgive you, Don. I forgave you a long time ago."

## USING YOUR INSIGHT

Do you have insight? You do if you have received Jesus Christ as Lord. With Him enthroned in your life, you can see yourself, as well as situations you encounter, in a whole new light.

Have you taken a critical look at yourself and found Christ to be in you? If so, take another look—an accepting one. After all, **God** has accepted you. Even if you have stumbled and fallen, He has not changed His assessment.

A verse almost buried in a deep prophetic passage in Daniel may help explain why the One who knows your failures still accepts you as you are. It says, "And some of those who have insight will fall, in order to refine, purge, and make them pure, until the end time" (11:35 NAS).

What you see as failure, God sees as "spring cleaning." The fact that He's allowed you to fall doesn't mean He's given up on you. In fact, it means just the opposite. It means He views you as someone worth saving and redoing. It means He's still at work molding you into the new you He's created you to be.

Have you ever gotten smack in the middle of a major clean-up job and thought, What a mess! When you've pulled everything out of an untidy closet, it may appear you have failed to improve your home. Yet that "failure" is your means to getting the closet orderly and useable again.

In the same way, any disarray in your life right now may mean

God is ridding you of ungodliness hidden deep in places you would never think to look. He is using your failures as a means to an end. No matter how devastating, those failures are not the end. Your falls, unlike the ultimate fall of those who choose to live apart from Christ, are temporary. At the last, all God's children will stand.

Knowing that, use the insight God gives everyone in whom He lives. Take a fresh look at yourself. Determine to see yourself as He sees you, to think of yourself as He thinks of you, to accept yourself as He accepts you.

Why?

Some strings of Christmas lights are so made that one loose bulb causes all the lights to go out. In dealing with failure, you have already tightened a number of "loose bulbs." You've looked backward and dealt with sins and false supports in your life. You've looked upward and dealt with your attitude toward God. You've looked inward and made sure of your relationship to Him. You can short-circuit everything, however, by failing to deal with your attitude toward yourself.

Have you decided "I'm a failure" because of recent events in your life? If so, be warned: You tend to become who you think you are. Although destined to live in victory, you will stay in defeat if you think of yourself as defeated.

Choose, therefore, to be who God says you are. Accept yourself as human, unique, and transformed.

### You're Human

David said, "By my God I can leap over a wall" (Psalm 18:29 NAS). David also said, "I am bent over . . . I am worn out and utterly crushed" (Psalm 38:6, 8 TEV).

If, in trying to "leap over" a wall or two, you've ended up flat on your face, it doesn't mean you are a bad or inadequate person. It means you're a person. You have limitations. Wall-leaping David smashed his nose a couple of times trying to go over the top, too.

You can fail, yet still retain and even bolster your self-esteem. How? By admitting before you fall, "I'm capable of failing." By being quick to say when you've blown it, "I've failed." By refusing to say, no matter what, "I'm a failure."

God Almighty created you. When you received Christ, He created you anew. He is still at work in you, mending the flaws, polishing the rough edges, reworking the places that don't meet His high standards. He has promised to perfect what He has begun in you.

In accepting yourself as human, you honor your Creator. You admit you haven't arrived yet. In labeling yourself a failure, you announce you will never arrive. You admit your Maker has blown it.

When Jan, from chapter 2, went home from the missions field to deal with depression, a perceptive counselor forced her to come to grips with her own humanity. He told her, "You're not going to do everything right. You're going to fall every once in a while. But that's all right. You get up. You try again."

Jan had to face the fact that, while depressed, she had failed to do her job many times. Even more difficult, she had to admit that she had failed to get out of depression by herself.

As a result, she has become more aware of her value as a person. She has gained a healthy self-esteem. It is rooted in her realization that God loves her, whether she succeeds or fails.

## You're Unique

Look around. You will almost certainly find someone else succeeding where you did not. You may be tempted to compare yourself to her—and then kick yourself for not measuring up.

Don't do it. God made you unique. You won't do everything well, but you do have your own strengths, gifts, and talents. Remember, you've been hand-designed by the Master. You are capable of success as well as failure.

The only yardstick by which you can accurately measure your success is the Bible. Within the framework of its unchanging principles, you will find God's high expectations for you. You will not find room to excuse mediocrity, but you will find room to be yourself.

Stephanie, from chapter 4, thought herself a failure. The job to which she believed God had called her and for which she'd spent years preparing had not materialized. She was quick to write "Failed!" across her life because she'd told herself since childhood that she would not be a success, that she would never measure up to family or friends.

Why had Stephanie decided she was not as good as everyone else? She was overweight. Her parents had taken her to doctors to help her lose weight, but she could not get the pounds off. After her father's death, she felt no one would accept her as she was. She felt helpless to change. She told herself, "You're not any good."

Don't do what Stephanie did. Don't write yourself off in every area just because you failed in one. Don't even write yourself off in the area where you failed. Stephanie is now a trim young woman.

She has conquered the very thing that made her feel she would always be a failure.

In looking within, accept yourself as unique. Consider yourself capable of success. Make the unique things about you work for you. Where changes are needed, make them through Christ's power, in order to please and honor Him. Do not try to live up to someone else's expectations in your own power.

Begin now to prepare yourself for choices you will later need to make to go forward. Ask yourself two questions regarding your uniqueness:

(1) *Did I fail at a point where I know I am "weak"?* For example, feeling inadequate at public speaking, you may have tried to teach and yet became tongue-tied. You may have taken on a job you knew you weren't prepared for and not made the grade. Having never before witnessed, you may have tried to tell someone about Christ, only to be rejected.

If you're broken at a weak point, don't despair. The apostle Paul *boasted* of his weaknesses so that through them God could demonstrate His power. Paul clung to Christ's promise, "My power is greatest when you are weak" (2 Cor. 12:9 TEV).

(2) *Did I fail at a point where I thought I was strong?* Maybe you are an organizer, and you tackled a major project that fell apart. Or, you have a deep love for children and a knack for dealing with them, yet you haven't been able to have a baby. Maybe you have a reputation for honesty, yet you fell into dishonesty.

If you've experienced failure in an area of strength, remember the branch about which Jesus spoke in John 15. It was strong and flourishing, yet the gardener cut it back. Why? To force the living branch to draw more fully on the vine's life. To enable the fruitful branch to bear even more fruit.

God may be using your fall to do a similar pruning work in your life. If so, today's ugliness and pain will yield tomorrow's fullness.

Don't be afraid to get out your spiritual mirror. Be glad when you look in it and see—you. Your Creator made you to be able to succeed—in your own unique way.

### You're Transformed

On his deathbed, the Old Testament patriarch Jacob called his 12 sons together and blessed each one. He said of one son, "Gad, a troop shall overcome him: but he shall overcome at the last" (Gen. 49:19 KJV).

If you are God's child, He has pronounced a similar blessing on you. He has declared, "You will suffer defeats, but in the end you will overcome."

Though still human, you've been transformed. Now you're an overcomer. With David, you can say, "By my God I can leap over a wall."

You don't believe it? You're too far down? After a hard fall, the thought of standing, much less leaping, may seem impossible to you. But the very fact that you failed, or appeared to fail, sets you up to be the overcomer God says you are.

After all, to overcome, one must "come over" something. One must get the better of a seemingly insurmountable barrier. Through the ages, Christ's overcomers have been hurdling trouble, persecution, danger, poverty, and, yes, failure.

Amber had a lot to overcome. She had tried every church from Catholic to Nazarene to Mormon. By her mid-teens, she had experienced pregnancy and a forced marriage. Soon afterward, she became an alcoholic and a drug addict. By her mid-twenties, she had two children (who had been taken from her) and an abusive husband. She had turned to prostitution to support her own and her husband's drug needs. She was practicing occult rituals. She had spent time in jail.

During one jail term, Amber picked up a book titled *The Greatest Is Love*. She thought, "Oh, good! A romance novel." But when she opened the book, she found herself reading a modern language New Testament. She thought, Oh, no! but kept reading out of curiosity. In all her contacts with different religions, she had only once seen a Bible.

After reading that Testament, Amber knelt in her jail cell and asked the Lord Jesus to forgive her sins and to come into her life. After her release from jail, she joined a Bible-believing, Bible-teaching church.

Now Amber's life is a testimony that anyone who is in Christ is a new creation. She has overcome occultism, as well as drug and alcohol addiction. She has seen her father, her sisters, and her children come to know Christ. She says, "Jesus has dramatically changed my life. He has lifted the bonds of addictions, and He has blessed me so many times I cannot count."

# DEFEATING THE ACCUSER

Your testimony may not be as dramatic as Amber's, but if you have asked Jesus into your life, the transformation is just as real. The truth is just as powerful: You are an overcomer.

Yet, when you are still hurting from a fall and you eye the impossibly high hurdles ahead, a snakelike voice in your ear will often whisper, "You'll never do it. You can't."

How, then, do you overcome?

First, recognize that whisper as the voice of your enemy, Satan, who accuses God's children day and night. He who has tripped you is now trying to keep you down.

Then, realize that others have defeated the accuser. "They overcame him by the blood of the Lamb and by the word of their testimony; they did not love their lives so much as to shrink from death" (Rev. 12:11 NIV).

As you look within, see yourself overcoming in the same ways as God's people through the centuries.

## By the Blood of the Lamb

On the first Passover, Hebrew families overcame the death angel by brushing the blood of sacrificed lambs on their doorposts. Old Testament rites for purifying people, buildings, and objects involved sprinkling them with blood.

Now that the Lamb of God, Jesus Christ, has offered Himself a sacrifice for all, His blood is continually pumping purity and power through His people. How that happens is a mystery. But God's Word declares it does happen (see Heb. 9: 11-14; 13:20-21).

When you received Jesus, His blood began its cleansing and protecting work in you. That work goes on, even when you are not aware of it. You can, however, unleash the power of Christ's blood to a greater degree by expressing your confidence in it.

Plead the blood of Jesus over yourself, your family, your home, your church, and those for whom you pray. Make "impossible" requests for salvation or for other things promised in God's Word based on the shed blood of Christ.

## By the Word of Your Testimony

What's your testimony been lately? A testimony of defeat? Or have you disregarded your feelings and spoken the truth about Christ and your relationship with Him?

Your words, of course, spring from your thoughts. Your words also feed to your thoughts. By saying aloud what God says, no matter how impossible it seems, you can effectively reprogram your mind.

Replace words of defeat with words of victory in Christ. Here's how. Each week for the next eight weeks, write one of the following Scripture verses on a note card:

| | |
|---|---|
| 1 John 5:4-5 | Romans 8:36-37 |
| Psalm 129:1-2 | Jeremiah 1:19 |
| John 16:33 | Romans 12:21 |
| 1 John 4:4 | Revelation 12:11 |

Place the cards on your refrigerator or bathroom mirror or in your car—somewhere you will see them often. Read each aloud several times a day. When you can say them from memory, continue to repeat them.

Then, when the accuser begins attacking you (probably through your own thoughts), attack back by speaking God's words. Your "skirmish" might go something like this:

> "It's no use. I'm a failure. I'll never get over this."
> "No, I'm God's child, and whatever is born of God overcomes the world."
> "Ha! You're too weak to overcome a few little problems, much less the world."
> "Yes, I am weak, but the Bible says I will overwhelmingly conquer, not through my own strength, but through Him who loves me."

Remember, overcomer, you are scaling a high wall. Don't expect your thoughts and feelings to change overnight. Relentlessly repeat the things God says, and do expect that your mind and heart will eventually catch up.

## By Willingness to Give up Your Life

Early in Frank Peretti's book, *This Present Darkness*, two angels discuss a spiritual battle they see brewing. Hordes of demons are planning to invade a small college town and take it over. At the same time, God's praying people are marshaling His heavenly hosts.

One angel reminds the other that those who go into the battle on God's side will be hurt. The other angel asks, "But will we win?"

The first replies, "We will *fight*."

That is an overcomer's attitude. It's the same attitude Queen Esther displayed when asked to intercede with King Xerxes on behalf of her people, the Jews. Esther knew that to approach the king unasked could mean her death. Still, she chose to do so. "If I must die for doing it, I will die," she said (Esther 4:16 TEV).

God isn't asking you to hate your life. He's asking you to hold it loosely. If you see yourself as already dead in Christ, you'll be able to do that much more readily. Like the apostle Paul, count yourself as having died with Christ on the cross. Recognize that it is no longer you who lives, but Jesus living in you.

Then, if getting up after a fall means heading out on an apparent kamikaze mission, you will be willing. Like a wounded but determined soldier after a period of recuperation, you will be ready to go back into the battle.

## OVERCOMING AT THE LAST

Not long after Don wrote his family and asked their forgiveness, he received a letter from Eva. She told him, "I'm divorcing you. I want to go on with my life." Eva's rejection hurt him. He knew, then, the hurt he had caused Caroline and his sons.

He says, "I prayed about it and gave it all to the Lord. He revealed to me that Caroline was the wife He had given me in my youth." Don believed that if he kept his eyes on Jesus, the Lord would eventually enable him to work things out with Caroline.

He wrote her again. He told her Eva was filing for divorce, but he did not mention the future he thought God had in mind for her and himself.

The two continued to write each other. A strong, new relationship began to grow. After Don's divorce, Caroline visited him in prison, at times bringing their two sons and daughters-in-law and their first grandchild. Don says, "They knew I was a totally different person than I had been before."

Don walked out of prison 17 months after walking in. He spent several months in a "halfway house," during which time he and Caroline visited often. Early in 1989, he was released. He moved back to the town he had known as home most of his adult life.

On April 7, 1989, the day that would have been Don and Caroline's 28th wedding anniversary, the two remarried. During their six years apart, both had come to see themselves as overcomers.

And they **had** overcome.

# 10

▼▼▼▼▼▼▼

# Turn Outward:
# Look Past the Hurts

Because she's had three miscarriages, Renee treasures her two sons. Her husband, Ben, had to travel a lot during the boys' growing-up years, so she and her sons were often alone together. They grew especially close.

Renee and Ben work overseas in a seminary, training young pastors. They left the US when their oldest child, Christopher, was five.

From that moment, Renee began preparing herself for the time she and Ben would send Christopher back to the states for college. Years passed. The time came.

After Christopher left, a couple of Renee's friends insisted, "You must miss Christopher terribly." In all sincerity, she replied, "No, this is the time I knew he would be leaving home."

Deep down, though, Renee was anxiously awaiting the time, just one year away, when she, Ben, and their younger son, Scott, would spend a year in the city where Christopher was studying. She often imagined how it would be: Christopher popping in for supper; bringing over his dirty laundry; asking for a box of freshly baked chocolate chip cookies. He and a girlfriend dropping by for a cola. Christopher just calling to say, "Hi, Mom, what are you doing?"

Finally, Renee, Ben, and Scott arrived in the states. One month passed, then three months, then five months—and none of the things she had imagined happened. Christopher had his own interests, friends, studies, social activities, and church. He did not think to make time among them for his mother.

She would call the dorm. Christopher was not in his room—or was just leaving. She would go to the school cafeteria at noon, hoping to see him. That would be the day he skipped lunch to study for a test!

Renee recalls, "This was probably the most painful five months of my life." She felt more distant from her son than when they had been separated by more than 3,000 miles.

Renee felt she had failed as a mother. She and Christopher hardly communicated at all. She kept asking herself, "What have I done wrong?"

Now she realizes, "I was expecting too much from Christopher after his being gone from home for a year. He had become independent of me, but in one sense I had not become independent of him. Once a child leaves home, things are never the same again. But I was hoping that they would be."

One night Renee tearfully shared with Christopher her hurt. From that point, the two began working to develop a new bond. "Today, Christopher and I have a beautiful, adult mother-son relationship," Renee testifies.

# A COLLAGE OF HURTS

Hurts. They come in all shapes and sizes.

❏ Renee hurt because a son to whom she had always been close grew away from her.

❏ Patty and Caroline (chapters 7 and 8) were wounded when their husbands left them.

❏ June (chapter 1) was rejected by students she had crossed the globe to teach.

❏ Jan and William (chapters 2 and 5) were forced by fellow Christians to leave places of ministry.

❏ Stephanie (chapter 4) went home after seminary in defeat.

### Hurts That Cause Failure

People can wound you in ways that cause you to fail. For example, a person who wants your job—in the business world or in the church—can undermine your efforts to do that job.

Church members who objected to the direction their church was going conspired to oust William from the pastorate. Students who refused to learn kept June from teaching English successfully.

Wounds hurt most when caused by someone you think is a friend. The prophet Jeremiah knew that people whispered about him even while he spoke God's Word. "Even my close friends wait for my downfall" (Jer. 20:10b TEV), he wrote.

## Hurts That Contribute to Failure

When you are falling, people can watch you go down without putting out a hand to help.

Patty was lonely through the year of separation before her divorce. She missed having a husband. She suffered, too, because many people shied away from her. "People didn't know what to say to me; they didn't know what to do; and most of the time they just didn't do anything," she recalls.

Zedekiah, king of Judah, is best known for failing. A wicked king, he refused to repent and turn to God. As a result, the people of Judah were taken captive into Babylon during his reign.

Before Zedekiah's fall, Jeremiah saw a vision of what was going to happen. He saw the women of Zedekiah's palace being given to Babylon's royal officers. He heard the women say of Zedekiah: "Now that his feet have sunk in the mud, his friends have left him" (Jer. 38:22 TEV). Those closest to King Zedekiah let him hit bottom.

## Hurts That Follow Failure

People can walk all over one who has fallen.

After William resigned his church, fellow pastors would not associate with him. Members of his former church tried to prevent his pastoring another congregation.

After Jan conquered severe depression, people hurt her in two ways. Some did not care about her victory. She says, "I was so excited about overcoming depression that I wanted to share that with everybody—and not everyone wanted to know."

Other people did not believe Jan had conquered. "It was very difficult to convince other people that, even though I'd been through the depression, I was better," she says. "It was like there were two-and-a-half strikes against me in some people's minds from then on."

Job had the same experience. He testified, "My relatives have failed, And my intimate friends have forgotten me" (Job 19:14 NAS). Job's list of people who rejected him after his "fall" included his brothers, guests, servants, his wife, little children, friends, and acquaintances.

## Intended Hurts

People can hurt you with "malice aforethought."

The gang that raided Grant and Ruth's home intended, of course, to hurt. June's students deliberately thwarted her teaching efforts.

If you want a clear picture of the way humans naturally treat each other, watch children. Youngsters who decide they don't like another child will tease, ridicule, and even threaten without mercy. They will plot ways to make their victim cry. They will deliberately shut out the rejected one when he or she tries to join the group.

When adults set out to hurt someone, they may be more subtle than children, but they are often just as cruel.

### Unintended Hurts
People can often inflict great hurt without meaning to do so. Here again, children give a clear picture of the process. They speak what they perceive to be true with brutal honesty. Often stubborn and conniving, they focus on getting what they want, regardless of the cost to someone else. They will demand the world and then take it without so much as a thank you.

Renee's college-age son did not mean to cause his mother five months of anguish. He was simply trying to establish himself as an adult.

Church members did not know their affirmations that God takes care of His people hurt Grant and Ruth. Still, the hurt was real.

## THREE HURTS TO FACE
Whatever form the hurts in your life have taken, they have probably caused you to pull inward into a shell. Choose now to turn outward again. As you turn, prepare to confront three aspects of hurt: the hurts you have caused others, the people who have hurt you, and the problems that breed hurt.

### Hurts You Have Caused Others
You have already glanced backward and confessed the sins that contributed to your fall. But in confessing to God, did you also confess to anyone your sins affected? If not, now's the time.

Decide, too, if you have sinned against anyone as a *result* of your fall. Have you, for example, taken out anger and frustration over a failed ministry on your family?

Make a list (mentally or on paper) of those you have offended. Then, go to those listed. Take with you a precious gift—the words, "I was wrong. Will you forgive me?"

In confessing, remember, your goal is to heal relationships, not to make matters worse. To help attain that goal, follow these guidelines:

*1. Make your confession specific, but not detailed.*
Identify the wrong attitude or action. Say, for example, "I've lost my temper a lot lately." Don't recount every episode in which your anger erupted.

*2. Make your circle of confession as wide as the circle of offense.*
Don't confess to your Sunday School class the wrongs you did to your family. If you've had a bad attitude toward someone, but have not done or said anything to make that person aware of your attitude, confess it to God but not to the person. Otherwise, you may cause a worse rift between the two of you.

*3. Deal with major offenses first.*
Don (chapter 8) had walked out on his family. Before contacting someone to whom he may once have told a lie, he needed to ask forgiveness from his wife and children.

*4. Don't offer excuses or try to transfer some of the blame.*
Don't say, "I'm sorry, but . . ." Your job is to identify the wrong you did, ask forgiveness for it, and then stop.

*5. Leave the results with God.*
You may think the one you've offended has done greater wrong than you. Don't go to that person expecting him or her to respond to your confession by also confessing. If such a confession comes, welcome it. If not, don't be hurt or insulted.

Don't even expect the one to whom you confess to accept your confession. You may ask, "Will you forgive me?" only to hear, "No, I'll never forgive you!" If that happens, your reply may need to be, "I'm sorry you feel that way. I hope someday you will be able to change your mind." Don't snap back at the one who refuses to forgive. Continue to do what you can to rebuild the relationship. Give God time to work.

## People Who Have Hurt You
After a fall, you may want to avoid certain persons. You may have a strong urge to cross the street when you see Mrs. Trompalong coming. You may be tempted to roll over on Sunday morning, rather

than get up and face the crowd at church.

Instead, murmur Philippians 4:13: "I can do all things through Him who strengthens me" (NAS). Then keep walking in the direction you were headed. Keep gathering with fellow believers.

Refusing to ignore people who have hurt you does not mean sticking your face in front of someone trying to claw your eyes out. It does not mean ignoring wisdom and discretion. Assume, for example, that you have recently divorced. You and your former spouse are in a custody battle and still attend the same church. Church members begin to "take sides." You probably need to find another church home.

Refusing to overlook persons means that when you are thrown together with those who have wounded you, you do not act as if they are invisible. You try to bring honor to Christ by treating even your enemies as graciously as possible.

## Problems That Breed Hurt

Don't use your hurt as an excuse for sidestepping problems that need solving. When you are hurt, you may feel that facing a volatile issue is just a shortcut to more pain. But if you do not resolve trouble spots that played a part in your failure, you may prolong and even stop your recovery process.

For Renee, "The beginning of the healing process took place with my sharing my feelings with Christopher. I was willing to run the risk of showing myself to him—hurts, disappointments, and all. It was an open invitation for him to come close again. When he saw how I felt, he was able to be open, too."

In God's power, you can confront unresolved issues that have contributed to your failure. Like a pilot about to take off, go through (and commit to) the following checklist before heading full-throttle into any problem-solving situation.

❏ I will deal with the problem at its source.

❏ I will attack the problem, rather than people. I will say what I believe to be wrong without pointing accusing fingers at anyone. If I have to confront someone who has done a wrong, I will not belittle the person by labeling or calling names.

❏ I will speak "the truth in love." I will leave quietly rather than get into an argument.

❏ I will listen to others' points of view. I will allow others to say things I would rather not hear. As they talk, I will allow God to speak to me about areas or ideas I may need to change.

❑ I will be as flexible as possible without violating my moral convictions.

# HOW TO OVERLOOK HURTS

As you look *at* the aspects of hurt described above, learn to look *past* the hurts done to you. Romans 12:17-21 gives God's guidelines for looking past hurts. Those guidelines include both a negative and a positive side.

*1. Do not repay evil for evil (Rom. 12:17).*

When someone hits you, your first reaction may be to hit back. You may swing your fists or lash back with words.

Either way, God says "Don't do it." Your Heavenly Father sees and remembers every wrong done to one of His children. He will mete out justice to the one who wrongs you, just as He does to you. If the person is a Christian, sees his or her sin, and repents, God will place the full penalty of the sin on Jesus Christ. If the person does not by faith allow Christ to take his punishment, he will have to bear it himself.

Romans 12:19 commands, "Never take revenge, my friends, but instead let God's anger do it. For the Scripture says, `I will take revenge, I will pay back, says the Lord'" (TEV).

Entrusting your vengeance to God does not mean biting your lip and swallowing your anger. If you keep the hurt and anger inside, one of two things will happen. Either you will explode, or you will simmer yourself to death.

With a pressure cooker, you can cook raw vegetables in a matter of minutes. But you never start a pressure cooker and then run to town for a couple of hours. You turn up the heat, allow the cooker to work for a short time, and then carefully release the pressure.

God may allow you to get into a "pressure cooker situation," but He will not leave you there long without providing a way to release the pressure. As you vent your anger to Him, ask Him to rid you of it.

On the other hand, you may be a simmerer. When cooking, you *can* leave something simmering on the back of the stove and run to town for a couple of hours. (Although that isn't such a great idea.) Yet simmering is such a quiet process you can also burn your food and your pot before you ever know anything is wrong.

God warns His people about stewing over wrongs done to them. Three times in Psalm 37 the inspired psalmist said, "Do not fret."

Then, he added, "It leads only to evil" (vv. 1, 7, 8 NIV).

As you pray about your situation, mentally let go of wrongs done to you. Focus on God. Trust Him. If the one who has wronged you suddenly stumbles, don't gloat, "or the Lord will see and disapprove and turn his wrath away from him" (Prov. 24:18 NIV).

### 2. Overcome evil with good (Rom. 12:21).

We cannot overcome bad attitudes by making up our minds not to have those attitudes. Rather, God commands us to replace negatives with positives. Seek to conquer evil with good. In so doing, you will deal a deathblow to the temptation to repay evil for evil.

To start, look again at those who've hurt you. Ask God to show you what their ugly words and deeds reveal about them. What you learn may surprise you. A supposedly saved person may have never received Christ. One who has tried to pull you down may be deeply insecure. An insensitive person may be driven by selfishness. Someone who hurt you may have been trying to help but did not know how.

Once you have seen needs in your "enemies," ask God to show you ways to meet those needs. You may not like a certain bank, but if you invest money there, you will probably find yourself defending that bank should someone else speak against it.

You've helped rebuild your relationship with God by investing treasure in Him. You can begin a bonding process even with those who count themselves your enemies by investing treasure in them.

If people do not understand what you're facing or know how to help, accept their limitations. When possible, help them know how to help you. For example, if someone avoids talking about your experience of failure and you need to express your feelings, say, "I'd really like to talk about [name the subject]. Will you let me do that?"

If the one who has hurt you seems to feel inferior or insecure, try offering her a sincere compliment whenever possible.

Whatever the situation, you can pray for those who have hurt you. After the divorce, Caroline could not talk to Don, but knowing he needed salvation, she prayed. She discovered: God answers prayer.

## THE FINAL WORD

The bottom line in overcoming hurts is a single word, a word Jesus gave as a command: Forgive. Forgiveness is not a feeling; it is a choice. It is the aspect of love which "does not keep a record of wrongs" (1 Cor. 13:5 TEV).

In order to forgive, list on a mental chalkboard the wrongs a person has done to you. Then, say aloud to the Lord, "In the name of Jesus Christ, I forgive_____. I count the debt paid." Picture yourself wiping the slate clean.

As often as needed, remind yourself, "I have forgiven _____ _____ in Jesus' name." Think again of that slate.

When you forgive, you will not immediately forget the wrongs you've suffered. You may never forget. But you will be able to remember without anger or bitterness. When you have forgiven someone—and he does something else to hurt you—you won't find yourself dragging out all the old hurts again. The old hurts will all be erased.

Forgiving. It's another seemingly impossible assignment in the process of getting up and going on. Like all God's assignments, it is made possible by Jesus Christ, the One who lives within every believer. On the cross, He forgave—in the midst of unimaginable hurt. He refused to return evil for evil. As no one before or since, He has overcome evil with good.

You can look outward, past the hurts, through Him who strengthens you.

# 11

▼▼▼▼▼▼▼

# Turn Outward:
# Look to the Healers

Stuart was giving his sixth-grade class a test. Two students with learning disabilities left the room to take the test with assistance. When they returned, Stuart met them in the hall. Looking over their test papers, he became angry. The two had obviously had too much help. He confronted the students.

Later, the two boys and their parents accused Stuart of unethical and unprofessional conduct in that hallway. They claimed he had cursed at the boys.

Stuart was innocent. But how could he prove it? Other than the boys, he had no witnesses to verify what he had or had not said.

He was called before the school principal. Later he met with the principal, the two students, their parents, and an educational representative. He was under investigation for two weeks.

A regular jogger, Stuart went out one afternoon to a track near his home. Jogging usually provided him an outlet for stress. That day, however, it didn't help.

He kept mulling over the situation at school. He didn't believe he would lose his job. But he could be reprimanded. A letter could be put in his permanent file. His reputation as a teacher and his Christian witness were at stake.

As Stuart jogged, he noticed the cross atop a nearby Catholic church. His own Protestant church was several miles away. He finished jogging and, on impulse, walked to the church. The door was open. Six o'clock mass was about to start.

Stuart went inside and sat on the back pew. After mass, the priest walked back to where Stuart sat. "I'm Father Ray. May I help you in some way?" he asked.

"I'm just trying to sort out some problems," Stuart answered.

"I don't have much time now," the priest admitted. "I'm due at a meeting in town. But it shouldn't be a long meeting. We can talk later, if you want to wait."

Stuart sat at the back of the church alone, thinking and praying. About 10 minutes passed. Then, he looked up to see Father Ray walk back in. "The meeting was canceled," the priest explained.

Stuart began to talk. The priest listened. From time to time, he offered words of counsel. "Sometimes circumstances happen which are beyond your control," he said. "You can't change them. You have to face them. How you react to those circumstances determines what you will get from them."

Stuart left that small Catholic church encouraged. Today, long after being cleared of the charges against him, he still remembers the priest's words.

# HELP!

You've fallen in your home. A sharp pain shoots through one ankle. Do you try to get up by yourself, or do you cry out for help?

You've taken a spill on the way up the church steps. Someone reaches out to help you. Do you take their hand?

Your answers to the above questions will hinge, in part, on your personality. You may be quick to accept help from others, or you may have a more independent spirit. Either way, you will need allies—the right allies—in order to recover fully from a major fall.

Falls produce wounds, and wounds need care if they are to heal. They must be washed. They may need to be bandaged or set. Medicine may need to be applied. Wounds must be protected. As every child knows, they must be kissed.

A major failure wounds emotionally. You may be able to patch up some wounds yourself, but you will never effectively kiss away your own hurts. Someone else must do that.

Your Heavenly Father, of course, will hold you close and do His healing work in you. Almost always, He will use people to accomplish part of that work.

In chapter 4, you probed the dangers of trying to live your life with no support or with faulty support. Now, focus on finding the right support. Prepare yourself to accept a healing touch.

If you tend to go it alone, you can learn to lean where leaning is appropriate. If you tend to lean too hard on those who offer help, you can learn wisdom and restraint.

Look now at some likely and unlikely healers. Understand some types of help they can give. Learn how you can receive what they have to offer.

## TO WHOM CAN I TURN?

God may bring a variety of "healers" into your life who offer a variety of help. Those you most expect to help, however, may be the last to offer.

Use prayer, therefore, as your main means of tracking down your healers. Your Lord, who sees exactly what you have suffered, also knows who can apply just the right salve. Keep your mind open, your eyes turned outward, and He will bring those persons across your path. They may be just the ones you have been seeking, or they may be persons you think unlikely to give you any help.

### Likely Candidates

Most people pick a doctor with care. They want someone who can diagnose accurately, speak cheerfully, and work skillfully. They want a person who has their best interests at heart.

When seeking someone to help you heal spiritually and emotionally, be just as careful. Look for mature Christians who are filled with God's Spirit. Confide only in persons who have proven themselves discreet. Choose those who clearly seem to care.

Depending on your situation, you may need to visit a medical doctor. Physical problems can complicate or even cause a failure. You may need to see a professional counselor who has expertise in dealing with the problems you have encountered.

However, in some cases, you may find that a discerning Christian friend can offer as much or more help than a professional would. You may draw encouragement from someone who has met a failure similar to yours and has overcome (or is overcoming) the situation.

Likely candidates may be all around you. Or, you may feel you know no one who can help. In the latter case, try to broaden your perspective.

Consider approaching a Christian acquaintance whom you do not know well but have felt drawn toward. After a mental breakdown, Theresa (chapter 3) gained healing through a Christian neighbor who attended another church. The neighbor invited Theresa to a weekly

Bible class. There, Theresa found the teacher enthusiastic and the Bible study and memory work an invaluable help in restoring her mind.

Consider writing, calling long distance, or paying a brief visit to someone you trust who does not live close. James, a pastor, enjoys occasional visits with two former church members who have now moved away. They're ready to listen if he needs to talk out any ministry failures he may be facing. They have committed to him and to themselves not to speak with anyone about the things he discloses.

Acquaintances and persons who live far away have one advantage when it comes to helping you. They are detached from your situation. Their counsel may be more objective than that offered by a close friend. Distant counselors may be at a disadvantage, too. Often, they have heard the story from your perspective only. Be sure to take both factors into account when you listen to their advice.

## Unlikely Healers

Stuart is a Protestant. He would never have looked through a phone directory and set up an appointment with a Catholic priest. Yet, Stuart received a healing touch from just such a person.

The unlikely healers in your life are the ones you probably won't make an appointment to see. They are the ones God will put in your way by divine appointment. You will recognize them as they cross your path if you stay sensitive to His leadership.

As with Stuart, the unlikely healers God sends may be unknown to you before your meeting. They may be acquaintances you've never had a chance to get to know before. They may be persons you know well, but have never considered healers.

Stephanie (chapter 4) grew up wanting her mother to be different. After seminary, when Stephanie hit bottom, she could have ignored her mom's words, "You're coming home." Instead, she responded to her mother's offer of help. She began to accept her mother the way she was.

In so doing, Stephanie found healing for her emotions and for their relationship. She now says, "I love my mother greatly. She became my best friend during that time."

Don't assume someone can't help you because he or she isn't who you expected. If you're down and an unlikely person holds out a hand—unless you're certain God is saying "No"—reach out to grab that hand.

# HOW CAN THEY HELP?

Not everyone offers healing in the same way. Some give comfort by their presence. Others speak healing words. Some take action to help. Others give aid simply by being who they are.

## Listening

Proverbs 11:12 says, "A man of understanding keeps silent" (NAS). Some of the most effective healers have learned to keep silent. They come with a touch or a hug. They sit and they let **you** talk.

They know how to be quiet with a purpose. Their purpose is to listen.

Listening healers encourage you to talk out your feelings. As you do so, their minds don't wander. They focus on what you are saying.

Good listeners look you in the eye (but don't stare you down). Their interested expressions motivate you to keep talking. They don't break into a conversation with a totally unrelated story they've been planning to tell the whole time you were speaking. Instead, they ask questions or make comments related to what you have just said.

Listening healers give you the chance to conquer fears and confusion simply by expressing them.

## Talking

The people of Judah had been taken captive to Babylon. After 70 years, a small band of them had straggled home. Even before trying to restore the other parts of their ravaged homeland, the returnees determined to rebuild the Temple.

They quickly organized, gathered supplies, and laid the temple foundation. But enemy people living in Judah used threats and trickery to stop the work. For 15 years, God's people failed to complete what they had set out to do.

Then, two prophets began to speak out. Haggai and Zechariah didn't pull any punches. Both said, in essence, "You've failed. Now it's time to try again." They encouraged the people with words straight from God: "Do the work, for I am with you" (Hag. 2:4b TEV).

When people offer you healing words, those words may not always be just what you want to hear. They may sting, as did Haggai's and Zechariah's words.

True healing words are not daggers thrust at you to wound you further, however. They are like antiseptic applied to a wound. Although they may hurt for a moment, they prevent greater pain later.

Accept the sting of the truth spoken in love. Remember that those who say, "All is well," when all is not well offer no true healing.

If healers' words sometimes sting, they also encourage. They may suggest practical steps you can take and urge you to take those steps. They may offer to walk beside you. They may remind you of the God who will never leave you.

Healing words can be spoken or written. Several counselors spoke words that helped Jan recover from severe depression. Equally helpful, she says, were the notes persons wrote her, saying, "We're praying for you."

Of course, people—even Christian people—can easily say the wrong things. Your most trusted adviser may sometimes tell you things that are unwise or untrue. Some things that are true or wise may not be said in love.

Filter the advice of others through prayer. But don't quit listening. Why? Because "the tongue of the wise brings healing" (Prov. 12:18 NAS).

## Doing

Some healers minister by taking action. One person may pray for you, fervently, consistently. Another may meet a practical need.

After resigning from his pastorate, William (chapter 5) was working in a grocery and attending Trinity church. He recalls, "About every three or four weeks, as we would leave the church, one man would shake hands with me, and he might have some crumpled up one dollar bills or a ten or a five in his hand. He'd say, `Take your kids to McDonald's today so they can get a hamburger.'"

William still appreciates this one who tried to help him and his family live "normally" during a time of great upheaval.

Sometimes healers do their deeds anonymously. Patty (chapter 7) was struggling financially. After church services on Sundays, she would sometimes find a bag of groceries or an envelope containing ten dollars lying on the front seat of her car. To this day she doesn't know who put them there.

Patty especially appreciates the witness those gifts were to her four-year-old son Justin. Now a teenager, Justin still talks about the way God provided for him and his mom through the food and money left on the seat of their car.

However they do it, "doing healers" live out the Bible's declaration in 1 John 3:18 that true love shows itself in action.

**Being**

Some people can encourage you just by living their lives in front of you. These healers often don't know they are healers. Maybe they have taken a fall themselves. Though having every reason to be flat on their faces, they are up and walking again. Seeing them, you want to follow their example.

Peter became a "being healer." He had denied the Lord. Yet after Jesus' resurrection and ascension, Peter healed people just by walking past them (see Acts 5:15-16).

A being healer helped June (chapter 1) overcome failure in an impossible teaching situation. The healer, a young American woman named Sue, had come to work in the same school where June taught. Six months later, Sue was asked to be school director. Civil unrest in the country started about the same time.

June saw how hard conditions were for Sue. She realized that, while she herself might have ten years left until retirement, Sue had most of her adult life ahead of her. June says, "I felt so bad that, as a young woman, she was having to face all of this, that I stopped feeling sorry for myself to some extent."

Sue was a listening, as well as a being, healer. Regardless of what she was facing, she made time to listen to June's troubles. She and others helped their English teacher-friend get perspective.

Being healers are living proof that recovery is possible. They are a testimony to God's power and grace.

## WHAT DO I DO?

You can do what two Jewish leaders of long ago did. Zerubbabel, Judah's governor, and Jeshua, the high priest, were the two leaders who should have finished the temple building project. Hearing the stinging rebukes of Haggai and Zechariah, they could have taken offense. They could have had the two prophets silenced. They could have ignored God's spokesmen. After all, to agree with the prophets' message meant to admit their own failure. It meant admitting they needed help getting started again.

What did they do? "They began to rebuild the Temple in Jerusalem, and the two prophets helped them" (Ezra 5:2 TEV).

Like Zerubbabel and Jeshua, you can admit your need, share your burden, and enjoy the results.

*1. Admit your need.*

Others cannot help if they do not know you are hurting. "But they can see what I'm going through. I shouldn't have to broadcast it," you may protest. Yes, but if you seem to have everything under control, people may feel you do not need them. Some may fear they will offend you if they offer help.

You don't have to announce over a loudspeaker, "I'm hurting." Nor do you need to tell your plight to everyone who asks, "How are you?" But if God keeps bringing certain persons to mind and giving you a desire to confide in them, humble yourself enough to do it. Go to them ready to accept constructive criticism and to weigh suggestions.

If someone offers help without your having mentioned that you need it, think twice before refusing. God may have revealed your woundedness to that person so He could work through him or her to heal.

When you've fallen and you're hurt, admit your need by reaching for the outstretched hand.

### 2. Share your burden.

If you're on the floor and someone extends you an arm, you're both going to have to exert some energy to get you up.

The same is true when you allow healers to help you after a failure. Those who reach out or respond to you will have to carry some of the weight of your problems. They may have to sacrifice a bit of time, money, sleep, or comfort to help you. But that's all right.

Haggai and Zechariah had to exert a lot of energy when the temple rebuilding started again. They "helped" with the project, encouraging and assisting. They didn't mind. Most likely, they enjoyed it.

When the Lord calls people to a healing ministry, He equips them for it. You don't have to worry that you're overburdening such persons. The Lord will provide them strength to help you bear your load.

On the other hand, you can't drop like a dead weight into your healers' arms, although you may be tempted to do so. Indeed, admitting you need help can sometimes open the floodgates. You've had everything pent up inside and now—aah! a chance to let it all out.

So, you call up a listener every time any little thing goes wrong. You let the talkers make every decision for you. You begin to expect the doers' help.

Some who appear to be healers may encourage you to make this deadly mistake. These persons are really cripplers in healers' clothing. Cripplers enjoy having you lean on them so much they never get around to helping you stand on your own feet.

Before you let the pendulum swing too far toward this extreme, stop. Make sure you are still resting your full weight on God alone. Wait for His go-ahead before calling and unloading on a friend. Take others' suggestions and criticisms to Him, asking, "Is this what I need to hear, Lord? Is this what I need to do?" Stop accepting deeds of help when you no longer need them.

Let others share your burden, but don't roll the whole weight of your trials over onto them.

### 3. Enjoy the results.

"Dear Emperor Darius," wrote one government official to the Persian monarch. "You won't believe what's happening in Jerusalem. And you may not like it. The Jews are trying to rebuild their temple—and they're succeeding! They're using stones so big they have to be rolled. They're already setting wooden beams in the wall. When we tried to stop them, we couldn't. What do we do?"

Darius replied, "Leave those builders alone. In fact, offer to help them!" (Author's paraphrase of Ezra 5-6.) When the healers and those in need of healing cooperated, God made them unstoppable. The temple was completed.

When you cooperate with those who hope to help, you, like the Jews of Jerusalem, will find new strength.

You will find the strength to stand again—and even to go back into battle again. Ecclesiastes 4:12a says, "Two men can resist an attack that would defeat one man alone" (TEV).

You will find new strength in relationships with those who have helped you. The second part of Ecclesiastes 4:12 states, "A rope made of three cords is hard to break" (TEV). By looking to the healers, you will have created a number of three-strand ropes, each of them consisting of you, another person, and the Lord who brought you together.

# 12

▼▼▼▼▼▼▼

# Turn Outward:
# Tend to the Hurting

Peter had denied Jesus. Talk about a failure! Soon after his denial, Peter repented. Still, Jesus went to the cross. Peter's world was shattered.

Rising from the dead, Jesus appeared to Peter privately, then with the other 10 apostles. Even then, Peter was at a loss as to what to do next. He gathered some friends and went back to doing what he had done before meeting Jesus: he went fishing.

He and six other disciples fished all night in the Sea of Tiberias but caught nothing. Early the next morning, Jesus stood on shore and repeated the miracle He had done the day He first called Peter to fish for men. He shouted, "Throw your net on the other side of the boat."

Not knowing their adviser was Jesus, the seven complied. Their nets filled almost to breaking.

John cried, "It's the Lord!" Peter jumped into the water and swam to shore. When the other six apostles arrived by boat, Jesus fed all seven a meal of bread and fish.

After breakfast, Jesus asked Peter twice, "Do you love Me as God loves you?"

Humbled by his recent failure, Peter answered each time, "Lord, you know I love You—with a brotherly love."

Jesus then asked a third time, "Do you love me with a brotherly love?"

Peter replied, "Lord, You know I do."

Each time Peter declared he loved Jesus, Jesus gave him an assignment: "Feed my lambs. Take care of my sheep. Feed my sheep" (see John 21:1-17).

## YOUR ASSIGNMENT

Have you taken the steps suggested thus far in this book? If so, you've gone a long way in the recovery process. Once flat on your face, you are standing again. Your knees may be weak, your energy level low—but you're up.

Now Jesus has a sheep-tending assignment for you. He says, "Look around for some lost or wounded lambs who need your aid. Nourish and care for them."

"Wait!" you may protest. "I can't help anyone yet. I need to recover more fully first."

You may still be confused about things that have happened in your life. You may still be battling wrong attitudes toward those who have hurt you or who failed to help. You may still be looking to one or more healers for support. You may be unsure what direction to take next.

That's OK. God's plan is not that you fully recover and then help others. God's plan is that, like Peter, you finish recovering as you give help.

## YOUR METHOD
### Seeing with New Eyes

June (chapter 1) had failed in her attempts to teach English to a disruptive class. She was wounded both by the students' attitudes and by her inability to change those attitudes. Yet, turning outward, June began to see her students as hurting people. She realized national conflict was tearing them apart inside. Frustrated, they were lashing out at anyone in authority.

She began to do the people-tending work God wanted her to do. She didn't quit trying to teach English, but she did start focusing on meeting other, deeper needs her students have.

Most of those students do not know Jesus Christ as God incarnate. They do not understand what a true Christian is, much less how to be one.

June realized what a rare opportunity she and her co-workers have to live and speak the truths of Christ in an Islamic land. They can teach the Bible and hold chapel services. National turmoil has multiplied openings for one-on-one witnessing.

June wants to be the light of the world in a place of great darkness.

102

She realizes, "We don't have to generate the light; we only have to reflect it."

Like June, you can tend the hurting, even if you are still hurting yourself. How? By doing a new kind of fasting.

## Fasting a New Way

In a traditional biblical fast, a person abstains from food for a time in order to pray and seek God. Sometime during your healing process, the Lord may lead you to fast in that way. If so, obey Him.

In Isaiah 58, however, God describes another fast for those who have failed and are seeking a speedy recovery:

> The kind of fasting I want is this: Remove the chains of oppression and the yoke of injustice, and let the oppressed go free. Share your food with the hungry and open your homes to the homeless poor. Give clothes to those who have nothing to wear, and do not refuse to help your own relatives.
>
> Then my favor will shine on you like the morning sun, and your wounds will be quickly healed. I will always be with you to save you; my presence will protect you on every side (vv. 6-8 TEV).

Basically, fasting is a refusal to indulge yourself in order to accomplish a God-pleasing purpose. It's denying yourself something you want or need so that God may bring about change.

The kind of fast described in Isaiah 58 is a refusal to indulge in self-pity, finger-pointing, and malicious talk. It's a fast from negative things in order to do some positive things.

While denying yourself a pity party, you "throw a party" for others. While refusing to feed off anger and bitterness, you feed someone else.

When speaking to Peter by the Sea of Tiberias, Jesus used two verbs to describe what He wanted Peter to do. The first verb is translated *feed* (John 21:15,17 NIV). It carries the idea of a herdsman providing food for his flock. Similarly, Isaiah 58:7 commands, "Share your food with the hungry" (TEV).

God may call you to help some people by providing physical food. He may call you to feed others truths from His Word that have become real to you through your failure and subsequent struggle to overcome.

The second verb Jesus used in speaking to Peter is rendered *take care of* (John 21:16 NIV). It literally means "to shepherd." Shepherding includes feeding, as well as nurturing, providing, leading, protecting, healing, and helping. Paralleling Jesus' call to Peter, Isaiah 58:10 commands, "satisfy those who are in need" (TEV).

God may want you to help meet others' physical needs. Perhaps you can open your home to someone who has nowhere to go. Perhaps you can help clothe someone who has little to wear.

God may also want you to help satisfy emotional or spiritual needs. He may ask you to open your heart to one not easy to love. He may use you to clothe with Christ some who have been trying to get to heaven dressed in their own righteousness.

Your Lord may call you to stand up for someone who is mistreated. He may lead you to pray for a relative who is "past help."

The list of ways to minister is as endless as people's needs. The Lord will match what you have to offer with what another needs to receive if you will agree to fast—by spending yourself in behalf of the hurting.

## YOUR MOTIVE

You may have lost your zeal for ministry. You may have lost confidence in your ability to help anyone. You may have more questions than answers. You may have more fear than faith.

You can still, however, begin helping hurting people if you will get one thing clearly in focus: your love for Christ.

That's why Jesus asked Peter three times, "Do you love Me?" He wanted Peter to build his ministry from that moment, not on his own faith, not even on others' needs, but on his love for his Lord.

It didn't matter that Peter's love was only brotherly love and not godly love. God can take immature love and develop it. What mattered was that Peter focused his love on Jesus Christ.

When you serve others out of love for Christ, you will be able to overcome lost confidence, lost zeal, doubts, and fears. When you serve others out of love for Christ, you will not be devastated if your efforts to help are rebuffed or accepted without a thank you. When you serve others out of love for Christ, you will point those who look at you to Him.

The Lord Jesus is not asking you, "Do you want to get busy helping others?" He is asking, "Do you love Me?"

# YOUR PROSPECTS

"Lord, You know I love You. I'll tend the hurting. But how do I know whom to help?"

Such a prayer can be your first step toward finding the ones whose lives God wants you to touch. He Who is faithful to bring the right healers across your path will also direct your way to those whom you can help heal

## Those Who Have Hurt You

Be ready: God may want you to tend someone who has hurt you.

After Theresa (chapter 3) was released from a mental institution, her husband continued doing what he had done before she went in. "He worked all day, came home, did chores, and then went to the neighbor's house," Theresa recalls. "The only thing he wanted from me was a physical relationship—to be his maid and do his bidding."

Months passed. God was doing His healing work in Theresa. Then, her husband learned he had cancer. Doctors gave him only two to three months to live. Knowing he was not a Christian, she begged the Lord to prolong his life.

He lived nearly four years. Theresa says, "During this time the Lord gave me a great amount of agape love for my husband. Despite the cost or circumstance, I determined to be there to help him."

She began working outside the home to help support the family and pay the mounting medical bills. She stayed at her husband's side through 11 operations, 40 cobalt treatments, and over 1,000 chemotherapy treatments. She was with him when he made his deathbed profession of faith in Christ.

## The Near But Unnoticed

Someone nearby may need you. It may be a family member or friend. It may be someone you don't know well. It may be someone you did not realize was hurting or never dreamed you could help. Whoever it is, God will open the way for your lives to link if you will be sensitive to His leading.

As Patty (chapter 7) went through the trauma of divorce and others ministered to her, she became aware of Miss Emma, an elderly woman who lived just a few houses away from the church. Miss Emma walked to church services every Sunday morning. She did not come on Sunday nights because she feared walking home in the dark.

Miss Emma did a lot of crocheting and other crafts. She did not have any family, nor did she have much money. Most of the time, she stayed home alone.

Patty and Justin began giving Miss Emma rides home on Sunday nights. Every week, Miss Emma insisted that the two come in for a few minutes. She gave Justin milk and cookies. Most weeks, she gave him a small present she had made for him. At Christmas, she crocheted Patty a dainty pocketbook.

Miss Emma has since died. Patty has remarried and moved away. But she still treasures the pocketbook and the memories it brings of one whom she was able to help while struggling to overcome a failed marriage.

### The Long-Distance Touch

Some persons God intends for you to help may live out of town. Distance is no barrier to Him. He can put you in touch through phone calls or letters; He can arrange visits to bring the hurting to you. Or He can take you to them—if you will let Him.

After her husband's death, Theresa set out long distance to help others. In fact, she left home permanently. She has ministered to women in crises in two states. Those she now works with live temporarily in a Christian shelter.

She says, "Many of the problems our ladies are facing I have faced. It is a joy to be able to share the Scriptures that have helped me so many times. Many times, I have had the privilege of leading one of our ladies to the Lord Jesus and of seeing her baptized into a local church.

"I'm thankful for a mighty God who is real, who saves, molds, and remolds us, making us vessels fit for the Master's use."

## YOUR DIVIDENDS

When hurting women tell Stephanie (chapter 4), "I've lost my home," she can say, "I've been there." When they admit, "I dread getting out of bed and walking the streets to look for a job," she can say, "I understand." When they cry, "I feel like giving up," she can answer, "I felt that way, too. And let me tell you about the One Who helped me."

"[God] helps us in all our troubles, so that we are able to help others who have all kinds of troubles, using the same help that we ourselves have received from God" (2 Cor. 1:4 TEV).

In your life, as in Stephanie's, Theresa's, Patty's, and June's, God has worked to help you overcome failure or apparent failure. Part of

His purpose is that you use what He has taught you to tend someone else who is hurting.

But the flow doesn't stop there. The Greek word translated *help* (2 Cor. 1:4 TEV) is rendered *comfort* in other versions. It literally means "to call to one's side." It often carries the idea "to call to one's aid." In the Bible, the term can indicate "to beseech" or "to encourage," "to call for" or "to console."

It's a boomerang word. As you offer others help (encouragement, consolation, comfort), you will also receive help.

Patty's divorce was final in February 1980. In July 1981, she traveled to another state to spend a month establishing a Christian singles ministry.

Long before agreeing to go, Patty heard God's call in every Christian song, sermon, or Bible study. She thought of a million reasons why she should not go. Yet, she told the Lord, "I'm willing."

As she relied on God to lead her, every problem was worked out. The Lord supplied her financial needs. He provided care for her son. She was able to take vacation time she had saved up at her job.

Patty's long-distance ministry brought her great joy. She says, "I think other people saw it in my life. Everyone told me how different I seemed." In turning outward to help others, she found herself renewed.

## YOUR CHOICE

Elizabeth and Walt were married soon after college days. They were happy and very much in love.

Walt began attending seminary and pastoring his first church. They had their first child. Soon, stress dominated their marriage.

The two had problems communicating but because of pride did not seek help. After all, they were the pastor and pastor's wife. They were supposed to be examples—not have problems. And besides, they thought, "To whom could we talk in confidence?"

As they served in their second and third churches and had their third child, they shouldered more and more responsibilities. They understood each other less and less.

By then, Elizabeth admits, "There was a certain pattern of negative communication. We were counseling others with problems but unable to help ourselves. It was like a merry-go-round."

Then, Elizabeth and Walt accepted faculty and staff positions in a seminary. Once there, they counseled, taught, and preached about marriage and the family even more than before.

"During those years, I felt like a fraud," explains Elizabeth. "We taught one thing and lived another."

Both partners knew their marriage was not what it should be, but each sought solutions in different ways. Elizabeth wanted to seek marriage counseling, while Walt began a quest to learn communication skills.

The couple decided to get professional training in marriage counseling and enrichment. At a training retreat, the retreat directors confronted the two, strongly suggesting that both needed help badly before they could help anyone else.

When confronted, Walt agreed to have counseling. Elizabeth says, "This was our breakthrough—the beginning of facing and admitting our failure and then being open to do something about it."

She now realizes that even Christian leaders sometimes get themselves into behavior patterns they cannot change without the help of a professional. She regrets that she and Walt were married almost 20 years before they made the choice to get that help. She declares, "You are not weak or less Christian to seek help when it is needed."

Working with some excellent marriage counselors, Walt and Elizabeth have overcome many of their problems. Today, the two have a wonderful, supportive, caring relationship. They are still striving to improve in areas where they have been weak. At the same time, they are choosing to share what they have learned with others. They accept many speaking engagements, preaching opportunities, and marriage enrichment retreats in hopes of helping other couples avoid some of the pitfalls and problems they have experienced.

If you choose to obey God by tending the hurting, you will not suddenly find yourself on Easy Street. When Jesus told Peter, "Tend My sheep," He warned that one day the going would be almost impossibly hard. Yet even on that day, the day Peter was led away to death, he did not again fail his Lord.

The hard times will come. But when they do, your God will abundantly provide. Turn outward, fast from your own desires, tend the hurting, and claim what Isaiah 58:10-11 promises:

> If you spend yourselves in behalf of the hungry
> and satisfy the needs of the oppressed,
> then your light will rise in the darkness,
> and your night will become like the noonday.
> The Lord will guide you always;
> he will satisfy your needs in a sun-scorched land

and will strengthen your frame.
You will be like a well-watered garden,
like a spring whose waters never fail (NIV).

# 13

▼▼▼▼▼▼▼

# Go Forward:
# Take a New Path

Holly sat alone in another woman's house and cried. She had failed.

Many children attended the small mission church where Holly and her husband were serving, but few parents came. Visiting the children's mothers, Holly found they had some free time each afternoon. She decided to start a Monday afternoon Bible study. Many women agreed to come.

Holly prepared for the first study and, on the set day, went to the home where the women were to gather. No one except the hostess showed up. The two studied the Bible and prayed together.

The next week, Holly prepared again. She visited the women a second time and told them, "We missed you. We want you to come have a part in Bible study."

That second Monday afternoon, she went and waited. Again, no one except the hostess showed. Again, the two studied the Bible and prayed together.

Holly visited the women once more the next week. She encouraged the older children in each family to stay home Monday after school and take care of younger brothers or sisters so their mother could come to the Bible study. They agreed to do so.

The next Monday, Holly went to the appointed place a third time. No one else came. Even the hostess said she had to go out that afternoon.

There in that home, Holly fell on her knees before God. She confessed, "Lord, I can't do this. I cannot get the ladies to come to a Bible study. I've done everything I know how to do. If You will show me how to do it, I will try again."

The next week, Holly came across a booklet titled *How to Have a Happy Home and a Healthy Life*. Published by a Baptist clinic, the booklet contained simple lessons on hygiene, child care, and nutrition.

Looking through that booklet, Holly realized, "This is what these ladies need." Most of the women did not have even a third-grade education. Holly could now see why an invitation to "Bible study" would frighten them. Yet, she felt they would be eager to learn how to improve their homes.

Taking the booklet with her, she went back to each house. She told each woman, "If you will come, we will study this booklet together."

The next Monday, five women, including Holly and the hostess, gathered and studied together. During the year, the group increased to 25 women.

Each Monday, after the study on nutrition and hygiene, Holly guided the women in a short Bible study. She focused on a verse that would help the women in their daily living.

She says, "During that year, I saw each of those ladies raise their hand and say, `Yes, I want Jesus in my life. I want this better way of life.' I cannot say that all 25 followed Christ. But some have come along the way. At the end of the year, we had five baptized ladies."

Holly believes God placed that little booklet in her hands at the very moment she needed it. She says, "It was like a new light on the situation to help me recover. It gave me encouragement and a fresh anointing."

## CROSSROADS

After a failure, any path you take will be a new one. Looking up from the bottom will give you a new perspective. Experiences of hurt and healing will lead to new sensitivity to others' hurts. Going forward now, even on a route that used to be humdrum, will be an adventure.

But "adventure" hints of danger; it involves risk. You may fear taking that risk. After all, the last time you tried to go forward, you ended up flat on your face. You may worry, "What if I take the wrong path and fall again?"

If you thought you had heard God's voice—if you thought you were following Him when you failed, or appeared to fail—you may be confused about how to know His will now. Your confusion may mount if the Lord chooses this time to remain silent.

And God may, indeed, keep silent. Often after a failure, at the critical juncture when you feel you most need to hear Him, He may choose not to speak.

His silence can be terrifying. Yet, it does not mean He has abandoned you. Nor does it mean He is no longer leading you. Instead, it often means He wants to teach you a new lesson. He wants you to learn to walk according to His truths, apart from any "feelings" you may have.

If you believe you need to get going again, yet you don't know which way to go, you have reached a crossroads. It's time to choose a path.

Before you do, though, beware that you will be pulled in two directions. Wisdom will beckon you, but so will folly. Avoid folly's paths at all costs.

## FOOLISH PATHS

Proverbs 8-9 draws a picture of people heading down life's road. As they pass, Folly calls out, "Come this way!" But, beware: Those who have heeded her cry "are in the depths of the grave" (9:18*b* NIV).

Folly may try to lead you onto a dead-end street or a road of retreat.

### Dead End

After a major failure, you may want to quit. You may be tempted to forsake your Christian ministry, life-style, and friends. You may feel like doing things the world's way for a while.

The pull in that direction is not from God. As you pray and seek Him, He may lead you to lay down one ministry and take up another. He may guide you to try a new approach. However, He won't tell you to run with the fast crowd. He won't tell you to leave the church. He won't tell you to quit.

Holly could easily have given up her efforts to start a women's Bible study. Instead, God showed her how to involve women in a study of His Word by first meeting a felt need.

Grant and Ruth (chapter 6) could have packed up and left their adopted country after their home was raided by an armed band. God did take the couple away from the scene for a time. Yet, they returned, determined to trust Him and give more heed to warnings He allowed them to hear.

Ten months after William (chapter 5) had to leave the church where he was serving, God led him to pastor again. Several years later, God called William to a new ministry in church education.

Whatever you do, don't turn onto the dead-end street, I Quit. God's plans for your life are "plans for welfare and not for calamity to give you a future and a hope" (Jer. 29:11 NAS). If you will go forward on the paths He chooses, your failure can actually enrich your life and ministry.

### Retreat

Remember Peter's fishing trip on the Sea of Tiberias? Jesus came out that day to let Peter know he couldn't go back. Jesus had called Peter to leave his boat and nets and to spend his life fishing for men. Even though Peter had failed, Jesus never canceled His calling. In fact, "God's gifts and his call are irrevocable" (Rom. 11:29 NIV).

That doesn't mean God won't sometimes lead you to change directions. Genesis 16 gives evidence of this. One day God met Hagar, Sarai's maid, by a spring in the wilderness. Hagar was running from an intolerable situation.

Abram and Sarai had failed to wait for God to fulfill His promise in His way. They used Hagar to try to produce a son. Once she conceived, she became cocky and began to despise her barren mistress. As a result, Abram allowed Sarai to mistreat Hagar.

Meeting Hagar at the spring, the Lord told her to turn around and go back—but not to go backward. To return to Abram's household, Hagar had to change her attitude. She had to humble herself, a forward step in her character development and in her relationship with Sarai.

God may call you to back up and regroup. He may send you in a different direction, but He will never signal retreat. If you hear that call, ignore it.

## WISE PATHS

Like Folly, Wisdom stands at the crossroads, calling to everyone who passes by: "Listen to my excellent words; all I tell you is right" (Prov. 8:6 TEV).

Where will Wisdom lead you? You won't find a map of your route laid out in this chapter. God's path for your life is unique. Only He knows it. But God does give some indicators by which you can judge whether you are heading His way.

Proverbs 15:19 says, "The path of the upright is a highway" (NAS).

Wait. Isn't the way that leads to life "narrow?" Yes. That "way" is Jesus Himself. But once you have taken God's narrow way in Christ, the Lord promises to broaden the road into a highway. He will not lead you along a barely discernible footpath, but along an interstate you can easily see and freely follow.

God's highways have three characteristics in common. They are paths of life, peace, and growth.

## Paths of Life

People commit suicide over major failures. To some, it may seem a way out, but it is not God's way out.

Other people, who may never consider taking their own lives, set out on paths just as destructive. A person whose marriage has failed may, for example, walk into immorality. The Bible warns: Immorality is a death trap.

A woman who has failed morally may choose abortion, the way of death, to "fix" the situation.

Those who have had abortions or who have failed in other ways may then choose other self-destructive paths. They may stop eating, start drinking, or become drug dependent.

Any path that leads toward death is a wrong path. Of course, those on God's paths do die. But, the path is much different. When you are traveling God's highway, you will have supernatural grace to face death. Also, you will not choose to self-destruct or to destroy others. You will not look *to* death but *through* it to a life that is far better. You will, in the highest sense of the word, choose life.

### Straight paths

Probably the safest sections of a highway are those that are smooth and straight, with no sudden bumps or hairpin curves. God provides such paths for His children. In Proverbs 3:5-6, He gives the prerequisite for traveling those paths:

> Trust in the Lord with all your heart,
> And do not lean on your own understanding.
> In all your ways acknowledge Him,
> And He will make your paths straight (NAS).

Pilots flying through clouds must depend on instruments to keep them on course. The instruments show whether the plane is turning or flying straight ahead, and whether it is ascending, descending, or level.

When in the clouds, pilots can easily fall prey to a condition called "vertigo." They may feel the plane is turning or headed upward, when it is really flying straight and level. If they adjust the controls based on their feelings, they can put the plane into a tailspin and crash. They have been taught, "Trust your instruments."

After a fall, you may suffer spiritual vertigo. To find God's straight way, you must avoid heading in a given direction just because it "feels" right. You must lay down your own understanding and trust your Lord. To fail to do so can mean disaster.

How, then, do you trust God to "make your paths straight?" A straight path is one with a purpose. It does not wander; it takes the most direct route from one point to another.

God's straight paths for your life move within His purpose, toward His goals. You show trust in Him when you head toward the goals He has set for you.

As you begin to go forward anew, take time to check your life goals, as well as your short-term ones. Ask God to show you whether they line up with His will. If you have never set any goals for yourself, get out your Bible and notebook and ask the Lord to show you His purpose and goals for you.

Once you believe your goals are in line with what He wants, use them to test any path you consider taking. Will that path move you toward one or more of your goals, or will it sidetrack you?

If a certain plan of action will cause you to deviate, even slightly, from the direction you believe God wants your life to take, avoid it.

Major highways through cities and towns often have frontage roads. A frontage road may parallel the highway—then suddenly veer off. It may have traffic lights, two-way traffic, and easy access to shopping centers. Turning onto a frontage road can mean losing momentum in getting where you want to go. It may mean getting sidetracked altogether.

God's highway is straight. Trust Him, and He will keep you on it.

*Level paths*

Dana got out of bed—and walked into a wall. She was on a cruise ship docked in the Bahamas. The ship was not sitting level in the water. When Dana tried to walk on an "unlevel" path, she ran into trouble—and pain.

Isaiah said, "The way of the righteous is smooth; O Upright One, make the path of the righteous level" (Isa. 26:7 NAS).

When you start forward, ask God to keep you levelheaded.

115

While out of the pastorate, William realized his teaching had focused on the Spirit-filled life to the exclusion of other important topics. On reentering the ministry, he set out to keep his teaching balanced.

Rita realized one January that she had talked about Jesus Christ to almost no unbelievers the year before. One of Rita's life goals is to witness to non-Christians as often as possible. In setting goals for the new year, Rita planned to include witnessing.

Your life can become unbalanced in almost any area. You can stay so busy doing things for God that you fail to spend time with Him. You may give too much time to ministry and not enough to family or personal growth. You may become so involved in furthering yourself or rearing your family that you fail to reach out beyond your home.

You can become so concerned with today that you never plan ahead. Or, you can stay so busy making plans that you never get around to doing what needs to be done today.

Whenever you focus on one area of life to the exclusion of other important areas, you create an imbalance. Whenever you omit any aspect God intends you to include in your life, you have missed the level path.

Ask God to show you any areas of imbalance in the path you're walking or are about to take. Ask Him for clear guidance on how to make the rough places smooth.

## Paths of Peace

If you've been down awhile, you may feel you need to run double-time to catch up. Such a flurry of activity is probably neither necessary nor wise. Give yourself time to build your pace again. Even in the midst of an active life, make sure everything you do rests on a foundation of peace.

*Old paths*

Stand at the crossroads and look;
ask for the ancient paths,
ask where the good way is, and walk in it,
and you will find rest for your souls (Jer.6:16 NIV).

Beware of groups that try to woo you with "new" truths. The ancient paths "where the good way is" are not found in the Book of Mormon or New Age philosophy. The Bible alone clearly lays out God's good ways.

If your path is to be one of peace, every step of your route must line up with the precepts of God's eternal Word. The more time you spend searching the Scriptures, the better you will be able to judge which direction you should take.

*Lighted paths*

When you travel at night you probably feel most comfortable taking familiar, well-lighted routes. The Bible not only lays out God's paths, but also illuminates them. As the psalmist wrote, "Your word is a lamp to my feet and a light for my path" (Psalm 119:105 NIV).

When you come to dark places along the way, look to the Bible for guidance. Let the commands and promises there make clear to you where you are and in which direction you need to go.

Armed with God's principles, start down the path you believe the wisest. Before you take the first step, say, "Lord, I want with all my heart to follow Your paths. This is the way I believe You want me to go. If I'm wrong, please stop me. I'm listening. You won't have to knock me down to get my attention."

As you start walking, keep a close check on your "peace barometer." If anywhere along the way, God withdraws His peace, stop immediately and ask, "What's wrong, Lord? Why is the peace gone?"

Listen for His answer before proceeding. Keep to His ancient, well-lighted paths and you will find yourself on the highway of peace.

## Paths of Growth

If you drive on familiar interstates only, you will never perfect some needed driving skills. If you travel too long at a set speed on a straight, level road, you may grow drowsy.

When traveling God's highway, you will find the unknown, as well as the known. You will find obstacles, even on the straight, level way. Knowing you may encounter obstacles anywhere along the road keeps you alert. Knowing you have not traveled a certain way before keeps you dependent on your Lord. In either case, you grow.

*Obstructed paths*

You may think God is leading you along a certain path—and then feel you've hit a brick wall. People in the Bible also ran into obstacles along the way.

Balaam was headed for a rendezvous with Balak, king of Moab, when the angel of the Lord planted Himself in Balaam's way on a narrow path between two walls. Balaam's donkey stopped, so Balaam beat it. He didn't see the obstacle, much less know that it was God's method of keeping him from the wrong path.

Job was headed the right way, yet disaster overtook him. He cried out, "He [God] has walled up my way so that I cannot pass; And He has put darkness on my paths" (Job 19:8 NAS).

Obstacles can take many forms. Interruptions, illness, bad weather, other people, your own attitudes, closed doors—all can stand in the way of your doing what you think God wants you to do.

Sometimes the obstacles are put there by God—perhaps to warn you to turn around, to guide you to learn creativity, or to teach you to climb. Sometimes your enemy, Satan, or his demons try to block your way.

When you encounter an obstacle, ask, "Lord, did You put this here, or did an enemy? Do You want me to go over this obstacle or around it, or to go another way entirely?" If God wants you to conquer the obstacle, He will give you grace. After all, He is the mountain mover. If He does not want you to go over the obstacle, He will redirect your route.

The Israelites failed to enter Canaan. God would later give the nation another chance to claim the land, but first they had to take a disappointing new path. They had to turn around and wander in the wilderness for 38 more years.

The people decided, too late, to conquer the obstacle that kept them from entering Canaan. They said, "We'll go up. We'll fight those giants."

God replied, "I won't be with you."

The Israelites marched out anyway and were soundly defeated. When God told them to go over the obstacle, they refused. When God told them to avoid the obstacle and go another way, they refused.

Don't be like those Israelites. When obstacles arise, use them as opportunities to listen to God, to get in on His plan, and to do it.

*Unknown paths*

Imagine you're on a new road—and you're blind. Isn't that how you feel on your spiritual journey sometimes? The terrain is totally unfamiliar. You can't seem to get your bearings. You thought God would act one way—and He acted another. You may feel abandoned, perhaps terrified.

When that happens, don't immediately decide you're on the

wrong track. Instead, stop and reach for God's hand. You may be headed in exactly the right direction. You may simply have reached a new stretch of road that requires you to be especially dependent on God.

How do you "cling to God's hand"? Confess that His paths are paths of life, peace, and growth. Keep His purpose and goals for you in front of you—even when you don't see how they can possibly work out. Keep His Word before your eyes as well as in your heart— even when the "light bulb" doesn't go on as you read or quote the verses. Confess your trust in your Lord, regardless of the circumstances. Seek His wisdom with all your heart, and then claim it, even when you don't feel you have it. Refuse to set out or to make camp apart from His Spirit of peace.

As you cling to His hand, cling to His promise:

> I will lead my blind people
> > by roads they have never traveled.
> I will turn their darkness into light
> > and make rough country smooth before them.
> These are my promises,
> > and I will keep them without fail  (Isa. 42:16 TEV).

Take the risk. Get on God's highway, and go forward.

# 14

▼▼▼▼▼▼▼

# Go Forward:
# One Step at a Time

Elesa was reared in a Christian family with a history of missions involvement. As a teenager, she felt a call to mission service. She took as her goal Jesus' command, "Go, then, to all peoples everywhere and make them my disciples" (Matt. 28:19 TEV). She particularly wanted to work with American Indians.

After high school graduation, she took tests required for entrance to a Bible college. She failed both the health requirements and the aptitude test.

Shocked and disappointed, Elesa decided she would never be fit for missions work. She says, "My mother instilled in me to always be optimistic, set some other goal, achieve it, and wait on the Lord to lead further." Still, Elesa found it hard to set new priorities and follow through with a new occupation.

She attended business college instead of Bible college, and she took comfort in Scriptures such as Psalm 136:23: "He did not forget us when we were defeated; his love is eternal" (TEV).

In early adulthood, she worked as a musician at two radio stations and studied broadcasting and diction. An only child, she took over operation of her father's business during a prolonged illness.

When her father was murdered by someone whose identity and motive were never discovered, Elesa had to deal with emotional trauma, financial hardships, and the selling of the family business. Through that time, she clung to her life verses, Romans 8:28-31, which say in part, "We know that in all things God works for the good of those who love him, who have been called according to his purpose" (v. 28 NIV).

She says, "My mother encouraged me to continue in local church work and pursue my love of music and poetry."

Taking a new job, Elesa met Raymond. Later, they married, and Raymond challenged his wife to use her knowledge of music and poetry to compose songs. She began to do so.

"With much study and the Lord's help," she says, she has written gospel and country-western pieces, marches, and folk songs. At this writing, eleven of her works are in sheet music publication; seven have been made into records. Seven have been transcribed into Braille and published by the Library of Congress into catalogs distributed to the blind.

Through music, Elesa has been able to "go and make disciples." Her songs have been used by mission boards both in the US and overseas. She and Raymond employ their talents year-round to witness for Christ to Indians and the blind in their home state.

Each year for 20 consecutive years, Elesa has spent two weeks doing volunteer missions work somewhere in the US. She has taught music training, formed choirs, and taught people to play percussion instruments. She has used music—including her own compositions—to communicate the gospel to the blind, to persons living in isolated areas, and to people of different races and nationalities.

In Houston, Texas, for example, Elesa created Scripture songs and taught them to thousands of Mexican-Indian, Hispanic, and Anglo children. Parents as well as children have been brought to Christ through involvement in the ongoing music ministry she helped start.

Since her "failure" to become a career missionary, Elesa has gone forward, one step at a time, into the calling God had for her. She advises, "His plan for your life *never* fails."

## FOLLOW A LEADER

You once were down, but now you're up. You believe you've found the new path God wants you to take. At least, you think you know what step to take today, and you have an inkling of where God ultimately wants to take you. In between those two points, many things are blurred. Still, you know it's time to start out. How do you proceed?

Why not follow the leading of an Old Testament go-getter named Nehemiah? Nehemiah appeared on the scene after the Jews' failure to love and obey God cost them more than 70 years in exile. A remnant of the people had returned to Judah and rebuilt the Temple; yet the walls of the capital city, Jerusalem, still lay in ruins. Attempts to rebuild the walls had failed. As a result, the Jews were intimidated by surrounding enemies and open to attack.

The returned exiles had "gotten back up," but they were not going forward. Nehemiah stepped out to show them the way to proceed.

## Use Caution

You may instinctively exercise a bit more caution now than you did before your fall—unless you're like nine-month-old Karen, who learned to walk by running and falling, running and falling. Or like one-year-old Amanda, who wanted to swim without help of floats or parental arms. Each time she'd strike out on her own—and go under—she would sputter, choke, cry, and let herself be held for a minute. Then, she'd fuss and struggle to plunge in again.

If you tend to take off at top speed, regardless, ask God to hold you in check a bit. William (chapter 5) admits he is now "not quite as outspoken" as he used to be. He says, "When you're boldly speaking out and you get your feet knocked out from under you, you become a little more careful about what you say and how you say it." He believes, "That's good."

Nehemiah would probably agree. A Jew in exile, he served as a personal servant to the Persian emperor Artaxerxes. From some relatives, Nehemiah heard about the returned exiles' distressing inability to go forward. He learned details of their trouble and disgrace.

For four months, Nehemiah wept, fasted, and prayed for his kinsmen 800 miles away. Finally, one day, Artaxerxes asked him, "Why are you so sad?"

Sadness in the king's presence could be punished with death. Nehemiah prayed silently and chose his words carefully.

He had been cautious enough to wait for God's timing. Yet, he was bold enough to lay all his cards on the table. He tactfully explained the problem and submitted his plan of action: "Let me go rebuild the Jerusalem wall." He gave specifics: how much time the project would take, resources he would need. Then, with the king's blessing, he set out.

Three months later, Nehemiah reached Jerusalem. At last! The work could begin. But no! For three days, Nehemiah waited. Then, in the middle of the night, he inspected the ruined wall.

Setting out on the path he knew God wanted him to tread, Nehemiah took each forward step carefully, deliberately. He bathed each action with prayer. As a result, God's hand was with him.

In today's fast-paced world, however, you may feel guilty and embarrassed by slow-motion progress. You may believe you'll miss something if you don't move quickly. Satan will use that feeling. He will whisper, "Hurry! Hurry! Hurry!" into your ear.

Yet God often takes time to work. Even when His call is immediate, He speaks it with a quiet peace. By refusing to run ahead of Him, you *will* miss something—wrong roads and unnecessary hurts. Listen for His voice and proceed with caution.

## Have Confidence

Sandra learned to water ski at 10 years of age. During her teen years, she skied often. Cautious by nature, she rarely crossed the boat's wake into the rougher waters outside. For years, when she saw a large wave coming, she would assume she was going to fall. She would let go of the rope and fall.

Then, one day, Sandra realized, If I hold on, I just might make some of those waves. She decided to try it. When she quit telling herself, I'm going to fall, she did not fall nearly so often.

Are you too cautious? Have you, like Nehemiah, learned to balance prudence with boldness? Or, like Sandra, do you avoid what you might not be able to do? Do you sometimes invite failure by believing that you probably won't succeed?

Nehemiah finished his nighttime inspection of the Jerusalem walls. He called his fellow Jews together and urged, "Let's rebuild these walls." When the people agreed to do just that, neighboring enemies started laughing and taunting: "You'll never do it. You'll never do it."

Nehemiah replied, "The God of Heaven will give us success" (Neh. 2:20 TEV). How could Nehemiah have such confidence? He knew who God was, and he knew what God wanted him to do.

As you move forward, plant each step on the certainty that your Lord is God. Focus on the truth that He "always leads us in His triumph in Christ" (2 Cor. 2:14 NAS). Voice your trust and confidence in Him.

Plant your steps also on the certainty that you are walking His chosen paths for you. You only walk in His strength when you are walking in His way.

Dr. Adrian Rogers tells the story of a young woman who, years ago, left the US to go to India as a missionary. The young woman soon ran into five problems:

❑ She stayed with two elderly missionaries who were set in their ways.

❑ She was unable to learn the language.

❑ She developed terrible homesickness.

❑ She found herself loathing the Indian people, instead of loving them.

❑ She caught amoebic dysentery and stayed ill.

After battling these hardships a few months, she decided to leave India. Then, one morning during her devotions, she read Joshua 10. Joshua had discovered five enemy kings hiding in a cave. Capturing the kings, he commanded his officers to place their feet on the kings' neck, claiming victory over them.

Seeing a truth to apply to her life, the young woman wrote each of her problems on a different piece of paper. She put the pieces of paper on the floor. Placing her foot on each, she claimed victory. Some interesting things began to happen:

❑ A young man from the US came to India for mission service. The two fell in love and married. That cured her housing problem and her homesickness.

❑ She enlisted a new tutor, and God freed her mind to learn the language.

❑ God began giving her a fresh and abiding love for the Indian people.

❑ God miraculously healed her body.

Identify the things in your life that threaten to keep you from going in the direction you know God wants you to go. Then, in the authority of God, claim the victory over them, and move forward with confidence.

## Be Consistent

"Sow your seed in the morning, and do not be idle in the evening, for you do not know whether morning or evening sowing will succeed, or whether both of them alike will be good" (Eccl. 11:6 NAS).

You know what inconsistency is: It's going great guns in one area, and letting another area lag. It's living in spurts—sometimes moving rapidly and sometimes not moving at all.

You may build up to an hour-a-day quiet time with the Lord, and then quit it altogether. You may insist on your child's carrying out a certain chore for a week, and then, tired of pushing, just do it yourself. You may make a "to do" list in the evening, work like crazy doing half those things the next morning, take a break at midday to treat yourself for getting so much accomplished—and then never get around to finishing the list.

Or, you may have your hour-a-day quiet time but spend no time putting into practice the things you read in God's Word. You may insist on one child's doing his chores—and let another child do none. You may busily accomplish the things you enjoy—and let the less enjoyable tasks slide.

Determine now not to live the rest of your life with a hit-or-miss, stop-and-start approach. Otherwise, you may "get ahead" like a student driver who moves by jerks. You may go forward like an erratic motorist whose moves cannot be predicted: She may or may not stop at a stop sign. She'll speed for a while and then go so slow that five or six cars are tailing her, trying to get around.

Developing consistency may seem impossible. After all, you have to work with your own memory, physical limitations, and moods and emotions, as well as with other people's demands and changing circumstances.

But consistency is no more impossible than any other quality God requires—and enables—in His children. Knowing that you will fall short, that He will pick you up and give you strength to try again, and that you will make progress, aim to go forward consistently.

Nehemiah had a major project on his hands. He had organized the whole Jewish population of Judah into a wall-building work force. But when a few Jews began treating other Jews unfairly, Nehemiah did not let the problem slide. He handled it the same way he handled his building project: with vigor and prayer. He showed consistency in wanting the best for his people in every area of their lives.

Stephanie (chapter 4) had come home, begun to rebuild her relationship with her mother, accepted a job, and was seeking God's will for her future. In many areas of her life, she was moving ahead.

But one night, while talking on the phone to a brother in another state, Stephanie passed out. No one was in the house with her. Panic-stricken, her brother called another brother who lived near Stephanie. The second brother traveled the 45 minutes to Stephanie's home and found her still unconscious. Finally, he succeeded in awaking her.

The problem? Antidepressants. Both brothers told Stephanie, "Get off those pills." She did. She knew that to continue taking them would mean destroying the consistent progress she was making in rebuilding her life. Stephanie says, "When I got off those pills, I could see a real change."

In order to move toward consistency in your life, be aware of areas of inconsistency. Be sensitive to God's nudges—or pushes—that indicate it's time to deal with a certain area. You'll never make much forward progress unless *all* of you comes along.

## Remain Constant

Nehemiah fought his way to the finish of the wall-building project. Along the way, every time he turned around, another problem arose. Enemies taunted. They threatened. They plotted to attack. The Jews squabbled and became discouraged. Enemy leaders tried to draw Nehemiah away from the work, then to frighten him into quitting.

But nothing stopped him. He kept guards day and night around the city. He kept crying out to God for strength. He kept telling those who tried to entice him to leave, "I am doing a great work and I cannot come down" (Neh. 6:3 NAS).

In just 52 days, the wall was completed. Why? Because Nehemiah practiced constancy.

You too will face hardships as you try to go forward in your personal life, family life, job, and ministry. Don't let the stumbling blocks stop you. Let them, instead, become steppingstones to develop tenacity in you.

Tenacity is bulldog determination to get from point A to point B, regardless of what lies between. For the Christian, tenacity is built on utter abandonment to Christ. It is carved out in prayer. It is strengthened by testing.

Jan (chapter 2) had almost given up. She'd waited four and a half months for the mission board to reassign her. Personnel at the board had told her, "We're sorry. We're trying. But we've had no calls for a women's worker in a Spanish-speaking country."

Jan believed God wanted her to be a missionary. But if so, He would have to open the way. Time passed. She was going to have to make a decision. She called the board again to see if anything had opened up. The man she talked with said, "Well, in another month or so we might have an opening in—Wait. Here's something."

That "something" was, to Jan, a direct answer to prayer. The same day that women at a missions meeting in the US were asking God to show Jan what step to take next, missionaries in a South American country were meeting and deciding they needed a women's worker. That country already held a special spot in Jan's heart. It was the place she had first learned to love the Spanish people. It was the country to which she had gone as an exchange student.

Three months after that phone conversation, Jan left for her new missions field. Set on following God, she would tackle each day as she met it.

Once you know the "point B" God wants you to reach, do not let yourself be stopped or sidetracked. Recognize that you will make mistakes, you will sin, you will be hindered, you may fall again. But go forward anyway.

Take one day at a time, one step at a time.

That's what Elesa did. Confused at first because it seemed God had stopped her from doing what He was calling her to do, she kept going. She kept going in God's direction.

For a while, none of the paths in which He was leading her seemed to make sense. But they were right.

## MARCH ON WITH STRENGTH

Dawn sat in a fast-food restaurant sipping coffee and reading her Bible. The verse God had given her for the year ahead was a strange one. In fact, it was only a line from a verse in Judges: "O my soul, march on with strength" (5:21 NAS).

Dawn didn't know that, in the coming year, she would face trauma at church, relocation, pregnancy, and severe job stress. She knew only that the same God who had defeated Israel's enemies would also fight on her behalf, whatever she faced.

She clung to that verse through months when it didn't seem she could put one foot in front of the other. At the end of the year, she was tired and a little worse for the wear. But she could say, "I kept on marching."

May you, too, march on with strength.

▼▼▼▼▼▼▼

# Postscript:
# The Beginning

When I started the research for this book, I had more questions than answers. While searching the Scriptures on the subjects of *failing*, *falling*, and *overcoming*, I saw that God had led me through the steps outlined in this book—without my realizing it. May I share a bit of my recovery process after one experience of failure?

The Sunday after learning my youth Sunday School students did not like my teaching, I was to teach—and Dee had to be absent. I used the time to ask the girls to state their complaints openly.

They did. The older girls, particularly, were very vocal and blunt.

I listened to all their comments. Then, I urged them to learn a lesson many Christian adults have yet to learn. I pleaded, "The next time you have a problem with a Christian leader or church member, don't talk about it to everyone else. Go to the one with whom you have the problem. Have the courage to speak the truth in love to that person."

I told the girls I didn't know whether I would continue to teach the class. I hadn't yet discerned what God wanted me to do. I explained, "If I do not keep teaching, it won't be because I'm angry with you or because I refuse to change my teaching methods."

After everyone else left, I stayed in the room and cried through most of the worship hour. A couple whom I hardly knew saw me there and came in and cried and prayed with me.

Later, after much prayer and after consulting with my husband and with an older Christian woman (who lived out of town and whom I'd found to be a wise counselor), I resigned the class. My decision took into account my pregnant (and thus very emotional) state and the antagonism I continued to feel from my co-teacher.

I called each girl in the class and told her my decision. I also told each one, "I love you, and I appreciate your honesty in our last class session." I meant both statements.

You may believe I made the wrong decision. My department director did. I worried that others in the church also thought of me, not only as a bad teacher, but also as a quitter.

Still, as best I knew, I had done what God wanted. Even today, I believe letting go of that class was God's will for me. Looking back, I don't think I missed God's will in accepting the class, either. How can that be? I don't know.

In resigning, I did not give up on ministry. In fact, two months later, my husband and I became part of the core membership of a new mission our church was starting in a growing area of our city. If I'd still had Sunday School responsibilities, we could not have helped with that venture.

I'm still writing youth Sunday School lessons, but I've switched the major focus of my writing and speaking ministry to adults, especially women. (Methods which that youth class considered juvenile, women love!)

As I healed, God planted the idea for this book in my mind. Studying passage after passage of Scripture, I began to catch a glimmer of what God had done and could do through people's failures, including my own.

I still have questions. I still have a few scars and bruises from failures I've experienced. But I rejoice to know that, in God's eyes, I don't fail—I fall. In His strength, I can always get up again, for I am an overcomer.

So are you.

Please, don't ever forget it.